Surviving the Computer Time Bomb

How to Plan for and Recover From the Y2K Explosion

MINDA ZETLIN

American Management Association International
New York • Atlanta • Boston • Chicago • Kansas City • San Francisco • Washington, D.C.
Brussels • Mexico City • Tokyo • Toronto

This book is available at a special
discount when ordered in bulk quantities.
For information, contact Special Sales Department, AMACOM,
an imprint of AMA Publications,
a division of American Management Association International,
1601 Broadway, New York, NY 10019.

Library of Congress Cataloging-in-Publication Data

Zetlin, Minda.
Surviving the computer time bomb : how to plan for and recover from the Y2K explosion / Minda Zetlin
p. cm.
Includes index.
ISBN 0-8144-7037-8
1. Year 2000 data conversion (Computer systems)
I. Title.
QA76.76.S64Z484 1999
005.1'6–dc21

98–49833
CIP

Printing number

10 9 8 7 6 5 4 3 2

To Bill, for sharing your life with me—
and for proving that a fascination with
technology can be contagious

CONTENTS

ACKNOWLEDGMENTS

Many people who are in the trenches of the year 2000 battle, and thus have very little time to spare, nevertheless spent a lot of it helping me understand this complex and dangerous phenomenon. I thank those whose assistance went beyond the call of duty: Irene Dec at Prudential Insurance, who helped me not once but three times (to prepare the article that became the first book that in turn became this book); Peter de Jager, consultant and coauthor of *Managing 00* (who has a talent for making this problem understandable to nonprogrammers); and William Ulrich and Ian Hayes, who put together the first of the two Software Productivity Group conferences I attended (which each turned out to be a two-day year 2000 education). As Peter advises: Go to a year 2000 conference; it will scare you.

Thanks to Martha Peak, former editor of *Management Review*, for recognizing that the year 2000 is indeed a management issue, and for helping to give this book its start; to Cathy Lewis, of C. S. Lewis Publicists, who arranged a wide variety of interviews and made me realize that there was more that I wanted to say—and more that people wanted to know about this topic; and to my editor, Ray O'Connell, and Sheree Bykofsky, my agent.

Finally, thanks to Andy Ferraro for providing some timely help in recovering data after a technological malfunction.

INTRODUCTION

Much Ado About 00?

By now you have probably heard about "Y2K," the year 2000 problem that exists in most of the world's computers. This glitch is the result of a universal programming standard that for years recorded dates the same way most people write checks—mm/dd/yy. The problem lies in using only two digits for the year. Software that uses two-digit year fields (that is, most software) understands the year 2000 as "00." This will mean trouble unless it is corrected in time.

You might ask, So what? So some dates will look a little funny. What's the big deal?

It would be no big deal if that were all there is to it. But it isn't. Computers are basically mathematical machines that use dates for a wide variety of calculations, and introducing an unexpected 00 into their operations is exactly the same as throwing a wrench into the workings of a delicate machine. The machine might stop working. Or it might keep working, but wrongly. Or, if you're very lucky, the machine might not do anything at all. These same three results can also occur with the year 2000 computer problem. We shall see that because all of us (whether we know it or not) depend on computers to work predictably and accurately, the second is by far the worst of these three possibilities.

Here's a true example of how one computer that kept working, but incorrectly, caused a big problem at a major company.

> The company had a simple—and very common—method for eliminating outdated customer files: The computer would seek out the account's last active year and then add five. If the resulting number was smaller

than the current year, the file would be automatically deleted.

In 1994, this system worked perfectly. It calculated that 88 + 5 = 93, and since 94 is greater than 93, any accounts that hadn't been active since 1988 were terminated.

In 1995, things began to go awry. When the computer considered accounts that were active in 1995, and added 5, it got not 100 but 00. Is 00 smaller than 95? Of course it is. So the computer deleted those accounts.

By the end of the year, eight hundred active accounts had disappeared from the computer. Disappeared mysteriously, as far as the company's management was concerned, since they knew they had a lot of irate customers but didn't know they had a year 2000 problem. Another twelve hundred accounts were deleted in 1996 (because 01 is smaller than 96) before the problem was finally identified.

It's almost impossible to know how a particular system will react to a date falling in the year 2000 or beyond until it actually encounters one. But we do know that Y2K can cause computers to malfunction in unexpected ways. We know, because it's happening right now. Here are a few more mishaps that have already occurred because of the year 2000 problem.

A financial company sold thirty-year annuities to investors. Because of the thousands of documents and accounts involved, contracts for these annuities were routinely generated by computer and mailed out to customers without human review.

As the computer calculated maturity dates that crossed over the millennium, it found a difference of ninety-nine years between the year it saw as "99" and the year it saw as "00." You and I can readily recognize this difference as minus 99, not plus 99. But many computer programs do not include a space for negatives and positives, any more than they include one for the first two digits of a century. Thus, the computer calculated the difference as (positive) 99, and the final values of the annuities were calculated over 129 years instead of 30—a difference amounting to hundreds of thousands of dollars for many investors.

Several thousand contracts were automatically sent out before anyone caught the error. Too bad for the company: The contracts were legally binding.

In a large office building, a maintenance worker accidentally set the elevator computer to the year "00." All the building's elevators settled (gently) to the basement. Why? Because the building's computer calculated that the elevators were many years past their required maintenance check and could not be allowed to operate. People who work in that building (and hundreds of thousands like it) will find themselves climbing to work in January 2000, unless the problem is corrected in time.

A manufacturing company used multiyear contracts when ordering chemical components for its plants, to avoid price fluctuations. In the summer of 1997, the company first began entering contracts with expiration dates in the year 2000 into its computer system. The computer system crashed, and it took several weeks to repair the damage.

Some Y2K Misconceptions

By this time, the year 2000 problem has been widely reported. Unfortunately, it's also very widely misunderstood. Misunderstandings about this issue can be dangerous because they tend to lead to bad decisions.

Misconception No. 1: The Year 2000 Is a Complex Technical Problem

This is a dangerous misconception because nontechnical business managers tend to think that the solution is to put their best technical people to work on it, and then leave them to it.

Actually, the year 2000 is a fairly *easy* technical problem. The reprogramming needed to replace a two-digit year with a four-digit year does not require a rocket scientist. In fact, consultant and year 2000 guru Peter de Jager of Brampton, Ontario, suggests that any employee who's reasonably comfortable using his or her computer can and should be trained to work on the year 2000 conversion.

What makes the year 2000 difficult is not the complexity but the *size* of the job. Millions and millions of lines of computer code have to be checked and may need reprogramming at every company, government, or other organization of any size in the entire world. To put this in perspective, Consolidated Edison, the New York City utility, projected in early 1996 that solving its year 2000 problem would take *ninety worker years*. Con Ed has since admitted that this projection was too optimistic.

Misconception No. 2: There's a Silver Bullet

OK, since it's a simple technical problem, then any minute now some software genius is going to invent a single solution that magically fixes everything.

One of the most dangerous misconceptions around, this false hope has led many business managers to take a wait-and-see approach to the issue. It's one reason both business and government failed to properly address the year 2000 problem while there was still time.

For a detailed discussion of the myth of the silver bullet, see Chapter Two. But the bottom line is this: There will not and cannot be a silver bullet, and anyone still waiting-and-seeing is only headed for disaster.

Misconception No. 3: Y2K Will Strike All Computers at the Same Time

Midnight, December 31, 1999, is indeed the moment when the year 2000 problem will do its worst damage. But it's dangerous to assume that you have until then to fix an essential system. The year 2000 isn't waiting until New Year's Eve 1999 to strike. Remember that the year 2000 problem can hit any time a computer program encounters a year "00," and that is already happening.

The first malfunction I described happened in 1995, and a slew of occurrences like it are one reason the business community first woke up to the issue that year. In December 1997, Cap Gemini America surveyed major companies and learned that 7 percent had already experienced year 2000 malfunctions. By March 1998, that number had risen to 37 percent. By the time this book appears, my guess is that most organizations with any serious computing power will have seen at least one malfunction related to Y2K. New ones will keep popping up through the year 2000 and beyond.

How This Book Can Help

Y2K may be a relatively simple technical problem, but it's an extremely complex and pernicious human problem. It needs to be understood by all of us, whether we are managers, businesspeople, or just ordinary citizens.

Here's an analogy. Suppose that the building that houses your company burns down, and everything inside it is destroyed. Replacing your walls, furniture, telephones, and even computers does not present a particularly difficult technical problem. Keeping your business alive during this period may be somewhat more challenging, though. Of course, you have insurance, and if a fire does occur, your insurance carrier is there to help. But consider this: Many insurance companies are now removing year 2000-related problems from their general coverage.

It gets worse. For this analogy to be accurate, we have to take it one step further. Imagine that the same fire that destroys your workplace also affects every other building in the world—at the same time. All your suppliers, your phone company, your travel agency, your electric company, and every other organization you rely on is hit. What happens then? How can you properly prepare for that?

A good question—to which there aren't any easy answers. Some people are busily building cabins in the woods, complete with their own generators and long-term food supplies. At the other end of the spectrum are those who dismiss the year 2000 problem as "media hype" and assert that nothing much will actually happen. (It's sobering to note that the people who believe Y2K is no big deal are hardly ever those with an in-depth understanding of computers.)

Neither response is a viable option. Instead, I believe there are things all of us must do to prepare our businesses and ourselves for the impact of the glitch, and to keep that impact to a minimum. In this book, I outline some measures you can and should take *now*.

Most of all, this book provides the nontechnical reader with a plain-English explanation of how the year 2000 problem came about and what its impact is most likely to be. Understanding is the most important first step.

SELF-TEST

How Ready Are You for Y2K?

The following questions are designed to help you determine how prepared you are to deal with the year 2000 problem. Unfortunately, many managers who think they've done everything necessary to prepare for the year 2000 bug will find out the hard way that Y2K can affect aspects of their business well beyond their own computer systems. By the time that happens, it will probably be too late.

The point of this exercise is less to learn whether you have the right answers to these questions and more to see whether you have answers at all. If you have thought about each of these issues and have taken definite steps toward solving them, then chances are you are at least on your way to dealing effectively with the year 2000 problem.

By no means does this questionnaire cover every aspect of Y2K. Even if you have handled every one of these potential hazards, there's no guarantee that you or your organization is doing everything that needs to be done.

On the other hand, if these questions start you thinking about aspects of the problem that you haven't yet considered, then they serve their intended purpose.

❐ *Have you performed "triage" to determine the computer systems without which you cannot function?*

This is an essential first step, but so far business managers have been understandably reluctant to give up any of their systems. Bad idea. Few, if any, companies will be able to fix every system, so some tough choices have to be made—and putting off those decisions means losing valuable time.

❒ *Have you worked out contingency plans to replace those systems if they fail?*

Some people seem to think that *contingency planning* means making sure the system doesn't fail. But it should be exactly what it sounds like: a way to get the job done (working manually, outsourcing, etc.) if, despite your best efforts, the system does fail. A lot of people and companies are dragging their feet. But if you don't have a plan for replacing the systems that you absolutely need, you are risking disaster.

❒ *What about the companies whose products you count on to keep you in business?*

Do you know how the year 2000 problem might affect their ability to deliver on time—or deliver at all—what you need? Have you done an assessment of their year 2000 readiness?

❒ *If your most important customers conduct the same kind of examination at your organization, will you pass muster?*

As the year 2000 nears, you will find an ever-growing number of your customers asking these tough questions.

❒ *What about off-the-shelf software you're using?*

Is it year 2000-compliant? If not, will the manufacturer provide a free upgrade? If not now, how soon?

❒ *Are you prepared to deal with the likelihood of a Y2K-related suit?*

The year 2000 problem is expected to inspire so much litigation that Y2K-focused law firms are opening across the country.

❒ *Which types of year 2000 losses, if any, will your insurance cover?*

Insurance companies asked all 50 states for permission to specifically exclude Y2K-related losses from their general coverage.

❒ *How will your company handle the year 2000 problem if a large portion of its programming staff leaves in the middle of the project?*

With the snowballing demand for programmers who can deal with Y2K, such large-scale defections are a daily occurrence.

❐ *Are you prepared for the possibility that myriad devices and "appliances" containing computer chips might also malfunction because of Y2K?*

This includes such things as automatic-locking security doors, VCRs, medical devices, to name a few.

❐ *Have you planned what to do if essential services that you count on become unavailable because of Y2K?*

These include water, electricity, phone service (both local and long distance), transportation, and shipping, among others.

❐ *Are you considering the year 2000 problem in all relevant areas of your business strategy?*

For at least the next year, every major decision—as well as most of the minor ones—should be made with the year 2000 problem in mind.

❐ *Do you know which of your systems are going to fail first—and when?*

By the time this book appears, most major companies will have had at least one Y2K-related malfunction. Other systems may not have trouble till the end of 2000, or maybe even later.

Surviving the Computer Time Bomb

CHAPTER 1

Everybody's Biggest Mistake

"People have been asking me when I think organizations will panic over their year 2000 problem. Most organizations moved beyond that stage long ago. For the others, now would be a good time to panic."

—William Ulrich, *Year/2000 Journal*, May/June 1998

In the spring of 1997, I met "Joe," an information technology manager for a retail chain. (Though I've changed Joe's name, the rest of this story is true.) Retail chains are particularly vulnerable to Y2K for two reasons. First, they sell finished products that must pass through numerous manufacturing operations and other steps, all of which allow opportunities for a year 2000-related delay to cause problems. Second, most chains absolutely depend on computer systems for such things as inventory control, ordering merchandise, and tracking consumer preferences.

In short, Joe had good reason to be concerned about the year 2000. Attending a meeting of the board of directors at his company, he brought a carefully prepared presentation explaining the problems associated with the year 2000 and how he intended to deal with them. But he never got the chance to give it, he told me when we met the following day.

"The CEO said not to bother," Joe recalled. "He said, 'We know we have to do this, so go ahead and do it. How much is it going to cost?'"

Joe gave the CEO his estimate of the cost, with low-end and high-end figures. The CEO responded: "Let's assume you can do it for the lower price. If you need more, let us know." And with that, he sent Joe on his way.

Joe's boss, I feel certain, believes he dealt with the year 2000 problem responsibly. After all, he acknowledged that the problem is real and was willing to allocate corporate funds to solve it. What more could his technology manager want?

A lot, it turns out. This just-get-it-done-and-don't-bore-me-with-the-details approach has done a real disservice to year 2000 projects throughout the business world. We nontechnical businesspeople have gotten very used to handing over our computer problems to technical experts and then leaving them alone to get things done. I've also heard technology people talk about "the business side"—meaning whatever the rest of us do. Both groups seem to feel their two areas are completely separate.

But they're not, at least not when it comes to the year 2000. Y2K is at least as much a management problem as a technology problem. Here are a few things Joe's CEO ought to be thinking about:

1 *Sponsorship.* High-level management sponsorship is the make-or-break element in any year 2000 project. If a company's top executives don't go out of their way to spread the word throughout the organization that dealing with the year 2000 problem is a crucial business issue, the chances of getting it solved before systems start to fail are nonexistent.

When I asked Joe what he wanted from his CEO, sponsorship was his first answer. If the top managers at Joe's company were not even willing to take a few minutes to hear about the details of this problem, how could they possibly communicate its importance to the rest of their organization? And if they didn't, he knew, it would be hard to get executives throughout the company to treat the year 2000 as a priority. That would make a tough job tougher; in fact, this is precisely what's happening.

2 *Loyalty.* One thing is absolutely certain about every year 2000 project, whether it is successful or not. It's going to take a long, difficult, and miserably unpleasant scramble to get it done. Ed Yourdon, a software engineer and author, describes year 2000 projects as "death march" projects—the kind that keep people up till all hours of the night in a desperate attempt to meet an impossible deadline. Yourdon suggests that IT managers seriously consider quitting their jobs rather than sacrificing their personal lives and health to such a task.

Most of them are pretty mobile already; according to some estimates, the average tenure for a chief information officer is three years. Since two-digit date fields have been around since the earliest days of programming, this means most CIOs have inherited, rather than created, the year 2000 problem at their companies.

That being the case, an IT executive in charge of a year 2000 project might well feel tempted to give up and bail out if an attractive offer arrives from another company—and with more and more companies getting desperate about the year 2000, such offers are multiplying daily. One IT manager at another retail company reported getting an offer to become another company's year 2000 project manager; it would have tripled his current pay. Considering all this, if I were Joe's boss, I would want to make sure he understood how highly his work was valued. Instead, when I talked to Joe, he was feeling angry and unappreciated.

3 *Liability.* Here's another thing we know about the year 2000 problem: It's going to be the basis for a lot of lawsuits. In fact, the lawyers are already lining up. Whole practices are forming across the country to pursue year 2000 claims, and though it's only 1998 at this writing, there are already a healthy crop of lawsuits addressing a variety of Y2K issues.

What if, because of a year 2000 glitch, Joe's company can't meet its business obligations and finds itself on the defending side of a liability suit? One defense is to show that the officers of the company were fully aware of and concerned about the problem and did everything in their power to solve it. Is the board able to prove that they were fully aware of and concerned about the problem? Is Joe able to say under oath that top management did everything it could?

4 *Business strategy.* This is the most important reason why IT staff cannot handle all elements of a year 2000 problem fix. The year 2000 problem is huge and will indirectly affect many different areas of your business. Not only that, it will affect the world economy and the very business environment you work in.

As a result, many of the decisions that need to be made as a consequence of Y2K have much more to do with business than technology. William Ulrich, a technology consultant, president of the Tactical Strategy Group, and coauthor (with Ian Hayes) of *The Year 2000 Software Crisis: Challenge of the Century* and *The Year 2000 Software Crisis: The Continuing Challenge*, said at a recent year 2000 conference:

> A bank could not justify a year 2000 upgrade of an assembler system because it was in a marginally profitable leasing division. It wasn't a strategic business for the organization, so they opted to sell the division to another company. The bank profited from the sale, the company that bought the division got a new customer base, which is what they were essentially buying. They avoided doing the upgrade because they already had a [year-2000-]compliant system. All they had to do was move the data over. So everybody won, and money wasn't spent to fix an outdated system.

Clearly, IT staffers are not likely to have the knowledge or clout to recommend such a step as selling a division.

Even if you know in advance that such drastic measures are not part of your year 2000 solution, some business decisions have to be made. They're likely to be highly unpleasant decisions.

According to the Gartner Group, a Stamford, Connecticut management consulting firm that has done extensive year 2000 research, more than 80 percent of all companies will have some year 2000-related systems failures because they will run out of time to fix all their problems before the year 2000 arrives. Some 30 percent will have failures in mission-critical systems—those that directly impact company survival.

"If you really feel your business is ready for the year 2000 but you haven't had any difficult discussions about priorities, then you're not there yet," declares Thomas Klein, a J. P. Morgan vice president at a recent year 2000 conference.

Triage, a term originally used to describe the process of selecting which wounded soldiers to treat on a battlefield, is commonly used today to refer to the process of deciding which computer systems are to be fixed. Is purchasing more important than delivery? Which business functions supersede others? Assuming that some of your systems will fail, which ones affect your business the least?

Whatever the right answers are to these questions, chances are your information technology staff doesn't have them.

Competing Priorities

My CEO stood up in front of the whole company and made a speech about how the year 2000 project was a top priority. At the same time, I'm not allowed to have any more money or any more people to work on it.

—A YEAR 2000 PROJECT MANAGER

In the spring of 1998, I ran into Joe again. In the intervening year, public consciousness about the year 2000 problem had increased dramatically. Y2K was the subject of a cover story in *BusinessWeek*, and segments on "Nightline" and "Oprah," among many other appearances. By now, I thought, Joe's CEO would surely be taking more of an interest in the year 2000 problem and its effect on his business strategies.

"No," Joe told me, "not really." In fact, now that his Y2K work was properly under way, Joe's company had decided to upgrade its computer systems in 1999—giving its technology people two major projects to complete at one time.

"I wish I could ask them not to do that," Joe said.

The advice from consultants and year 2000 experts is quite clear: *Do not undertake any other large technology project until after January 1, 2000.* But the response from technology managers like Joe is equally clear: We'd love to follow that advice, but management isn't willing to put everything else on hold while we deal with Y2K.

In other words, most people and organizations are now (finally!) aware that the year 2000 is a serious threat. But they still haven't faced up to the realities of dealing with it. Thus, the new year 2000 problem is one of competing priorities.

Like Joe's CEO, most of us know the problem absolutely has to be solved. We understand that there's an immovable deadline and that it will take a herculean effort to get even our essential systems fixed in time. We know all this—but we'd rather not have to give the matter any serious thought. And we certainly don't want to give up any of the other important things we're working on in order to make sure it gets done.

The Euro

The priorities dilemma strikes not only businesses and individuals but also governments. One prominent example of this is Western Europe's determination to begin using a unified currency, the euro.

What does the euro have to do with the year 2000 problem? Plenty. With the euro scheduled for introduction in 1999, the two are the biggest software conversion projects of our age. In fact, many programmers believe the euro conversion is an even bigger job than Y2K. Whether or not this proves true, we do know that each project requires massive amounts of reprogramming. But they're different types of reprogramming; there's little effort to be saved by doing both projects at once.

On the contrary, most people who understand the IT industry think introducing the euro at the same time the year 2000 must be dealt with is foolhardy—especially considering that even without the euro, we're already suffering from a worldwide shortage of programmers.

Given that the European Union has been talking about a single currency for more than a decade, would it kill them to wait until, say, 2001 to roll it out? In a recent survey, 54 percent of

British IT managers thought they should do just that.[1] But so far, European leaders have only reaffirmed their determination to get the euro out on time.

Closer to Home

"That's just like the Europeans to be stubborn," you say? Here's an example that's closer to home. At this writing, it's been just over a month since both houses of Congress voted sweeping changes to oversee how the Internal Revenue Service conducts its business. Nothing wrong with that—the IRS has certainly abused its power. But with its hugely date-sensitive software and its portfolio of interconnected and constantly changing tax laws, the IRS faces a particularly challenging year 2000 problem. Even before the new law, many IT experts predicted the agency would have a tough time getting its systems fixed in time to prevent malfunctions.

IRS Commissioner Charles Rossotti repeatedly warned that having to adjust to the new oversight system before the turn of the century would threaten his agency's ability to cope with Y2K. Nonetheless, the Senate approved the bill by a vote of 97–0.

Well, *Is* the Sky Falling?

One of the aspects of Y2K that makes it difficult for many business managers—and ordinary people—to formulate an intelligent plan of action is that there may be no good way to prepare for it if the doomsday scenarios come true and everything bad that could possibly happen does happen.

It's extremely difficult to make a rational judgment as to how bad things are likely to be. On one end of the spectrum is Nicholas Zvegintzov, president of the Software Management Network, who asserts that the year 2000 problem is no different from many other challenges the IT industry has met and dealt with in the past. (Zvegintzov, I should add, is the only person I've ever heard of who understands computer programming and still thinks the year 2000 problem will be solved before it causes severe disruptions.)

At the other end of the spectrum is Ed Yourdon, who asserts in his book (coauthored with his daughter, Jennifer) *Time Bomb 2000: What the Year 2000 Computer Crisis Means to You!* that Y2K will be a huge, worldwide disaster disrupting our lives so completely that food may be hard to come by. They even give information in the book for laying in up to a year's supply of long-storage provisions. A programmer and computer expert with more than twenty-five years' experience, Ed Yourdon speaks with the voice of authority when he describes how computers work—and might stop working when they meet the year 2000.

It's relatively easy to speculate about what can happen when the millennium bug hits. But what is certain to happen? The simple truth is that no one knows for sure.

This leaves all of us with some difficult decisions about what level of disaster to expect when preparing for the year 2000. Unfortunately, I can't offer definitive answers to those questions. But I can offer some advice.

1. Assume that the truth lies somewhere between Zvegintzov's sunny reassurances and Yourdon's direst warnings. I can't guarantee that the worst predictions won't come true, but I can guarantee that if they do, our lives will be so different from what we currently know them to be that most of our preparations will probably turn out to be useless in any case.

2. Make an informed judgment about which areas you think are likeliest to suffer disruption. This book is intended to help you to do just that. Then decide which of these types of disruptions are most troublesome for your business (and your home life). Plan to protect yourself in these specific areas, if you can.

3. Don't make the mistake of thinking that just because you know it must be done, it will be done. The Federal Aviation Administration claimed throughout 1997 that it would finish its year 2000 project in November 1999. That's way too late; it allows far too little time for the delays and snafus that are inevitable during an IT project of this scope.

   Then, in the spring of 1998, the agency suddenly announced that after a rocky start its year 2000 project was now well on track and would be finished by June

1999. That could still be too late. But, worse, it leaves a big question unanswered: How did the FAA magically shave four months off its monstrously large year 2000 project? I have a sneaking suspicion that someone in a position of authority told the IT troops, "It has to be done by June, folks, so do whatever you have to do to get it done." No one volunteered for the unpleasant task of informing this boss that the June deadline would be impossible to meet.

4 You can't rush the process. It's a natural instinct to deal first with whatever problem is most immediate—just as Congress did when it decided that IRS abuses were a more immediate problem than the year 2000. The drawback to this approach is that by the time Y2K *is* your most immediate problem, it's too late to do much about it.

As Stan Ostaszewski, senior manager of Millennium Management Practice, in Batavia, Illinois, noted recently, there's the rule of the school (you can cram and make up for the studying you didn't do all year) and the rule of the farm (no matter how hard you try, you can't make corn grow any faster). In most year 2000 work, the rule of the farm applies.

Unless your organization has already finished or nearly finished its remediation and is busy testing its newly year 2000-ready software, now is the time to give Y2K top priority. Other business concerns may have to take a back seat, and all other technology projects must be put on hold.

With about a year to go, it may still be possible to keep the systems your business depends on from falling victim to a year 2000 malfunction. But only if you face the reality that getting it done has to mean postponing something else you thought was important too.

Note

1. Survey conducted for software tool vendor Business Objects in 1998; additional information is available at www.businessobjects.com.

CHAPTER 2

Why Y2K Is Harder to Fix Than You Think

"If architects built buildings the way programmers write software, the first woodpecker that came along would have destroyed civilization."

—A COBOL PROGRAMMER

A few months ago, I met a woman who worked for a network television news program. When I told her I'd written a book about the year 2000 problem, she immediately responded, "Oh, they're going to find a solution for that!"

"No, they won't," I said. "They can't."

She shook her head, as if I were the worst doommonger imaginable. "How can you say that?"

It's frightening how many people—smart, sophisticated people with a good grasp of current events—seem to be perfectly confident that, just in the nick of time, a solution to the entire year 2000 problem will be found. As in a "Star Trek" episode, where Spock manages to create the new device that gets everyone back to the ship safely just as the Klingons are coming around the corner.

It won't happen.

This imaginary piece of software is what the computer industry calls a silver bullet, a sort of smart bomb wending its way through every program, identifying every line of code with a two-digit year, and automatically correcting them all. This description alone might be enough to make it clear why such a thing cannot possibly exist.

What do exist are software "tools," programs to flag lines of code that might contain two-digit years and help rewrite them to avoid the problem. Although many companies have used the term *fully automated* somewhat creatively in selling these products, the truth is that every one of them needs a human programmer standing by to determine whether what seems like a year actually is one. Most of these tools are very useful software that can make a year 2000 fix much quicker and more efficient. But as Y2K guru Peter de Jager once told me, "There's nothing that you can pop in on Friday afternoon, and when you come back on Monday it's done."[1]

If ever there was hope of a genuine silver bullet with which to shoot down the whole year 2000 problem, it is disappearing fast. There are literally thousands of ways that dates are stored and used within computer programs. No one piece of software can deal with them all—even if it were limited to just one computer language.

At this point, chances are no one is even trying to come up with one anymore. The year 2000 problem presents a business opportunity of limited duration—a reality the world's software vendors are well aware of. By early 1997, most year 2000 vendors had already switched the bulk of their budgets away from research and development in favor of marketing and sales. Their logic was simple: If they did not start aggressively selling the software they'd developed, they would miss their only chance to make money in this market.

Morgan Stanley computer industry analysts Charles Phillips and William Farrell identified this trend in March 1997 in a special white paper on investing in Y2K (see Recommended Other Reading). In their view, this meant the chances of a silver bullet ever appearing were "next to nil." Nonetheless, hope for the silver bullet has prompted leaders of both industry and government to take a wait-and-see approach to the year 2000, which is one reason so many of the world's systems are now far beyond the possibility of complete repair.

Is Rover a Date?

The very nature of the year 2000 problem is what makes it so perplexing to solve. To understand why, begin with the first step of the fix: finding those parts of a program that refer to dates. It sounds simple enough, and it would be simple—if one could walk up to a computer and ask it which lines of programming code contain date fields. Unfortunately, one can't. There isn't any obvious way to tell.

Remember that any program—from a computer game to a word processor—is nothing more than a set of instructions, and those instructions were written, once upon a time, by a human programmer. He or she expected to be the only human who would ever read those instructions. Or, perhaps the programmer wanted to *make sure* of being the only person who could read the program—thus guaranteeing a degree of job security.

Keeping this in mind, imagine you're a programmer, about to name a date field (a place in your program where a date is to be stored). You might name it something obvious like ACCOUNT_START_DATE. On the other hand, if you're planning to be the only one to use the program, you might name it **ROVER**, after your golden retriever.

Now, imagine that it's ten years later. You have long since moved on, and a new programmer is working on the year 2000 project. She comes across this statement: **IF ROVER > 60 THEN GOTO 1400**. You know the program is used for calculating bank loans, and when you look at instruction 1400, you learn that it sets a particular interest rate. But what is **ROVER**?

Here are just a few of the endless possibilities:

- **ROVER** is the age of the borrower; the bank wants to give a better rate to those over sixty.

- **ROVER** is the year the borrower's account was first opened; the bank wants to give a higher rate to those who opened their account before 1960. (Note: If this is the case, this line needs to be rewritten; otherwise anyone opening an account in the year 2000 or later will also get the discount!)

- Your program is calculating mortgages, and **ROVER** is the year the house in question was built; the bank wants to give a discount for newer houses.

- Or, **ROVER** is the age of the house; the bank wants to give a discount for *older* houses.

And on, and on . . . but you get the idea.

It Gets Worse

What I've just described is a well-functioning, clearly written (though not well-documented) piece of software. The year 2000 would be difficult enough to deal with if every piece of programming met that description. Unfortunately, they don't. Those of us who use computers and see them functioning smoothly (most of the time) have difficulty imagining how disorganized the inside of a program can be. Here are some of the messes many programmers have to clean up before they can even start tackling the year 2000 problem:

- *"Spaghetti" code.* Programmers use "**IF . . . THEN**" and "**GOTO**" and other instructions to jump around inside a program. For example: **IF** (the outstanding balance was paid today) **THEN** (set balance to zero) **ELSE** (calculate interest owed for today); then **IF** (number of days since last payment received is greater than 30) **GOTO** (instructions that mail out a reminder notice).

  This allows the program to deal correctly with a wide variety of possibilities. However, as the program is updated and adjusted over time, the accumulation of **IF . . . THENS** and **GOTOS** can become so tangled that it's impossible to tell where it begins and ends. Thus the term "spaghetti." Year 2000 repairs are likely to have repercussions throughout a program, and dates can pop up anywhere. This means that spaghetti code has to be dealt with somehow in the course of a Y2K project.

- *Dead code.* Dead code is programming that exists on your computer but isn't actually doing anything. Why would such code be there? Because the program has been changed or customized over time, and although the new programming bypasses the dead code, it has not actually been deleted. Needless to say, it's a waste of valuable programmer time and energy to fix the year 2000 problem in dead code—and if you're paying an outside vendor to work on the problem, it's a waste of money as well.

- *Lost source code.* Source code is the actual programming instructions the programmer wrote in COBOL, FORTRAN, UNIX, or some other programming language. This is then automatically translated into "machine code," which runs on the actual computer. To the human eye, machine code looks like this:

00000780 C088D503 6038C100 07725810 C05C07F1
00000790 5800C084 5000D260 5810C07C 07F15800
000007A0 D2385000 D260D203 6104C0EC 41106030
000007B0 5010D278 41106091 5010D27C 9680D27C

Machine code is all that's needed for a program to work perfectly well. But even an accomplished programmer can't tell by looking at them what these instructions say, let alone whether they involve dates. In some cases where the original programmer has moved on, the source code is nowhere to be found.

Missing source code is a surprisingly common problem; most companies with any history of computer use have lost at least some of their source. Some companies are finding that 25 percent of their source code is missing. Overall, the Gartner Group estimates that about 10 percent of the world's software has missing source code.

Organizations with lost source code face an unpleasant choice in dealing with the year 2000 problem. They must either jettison the existing programs and write new ones, or hire a vendor to reconstruct the source code from machine code, a difficult process. Either option is expensive and time-consuming.

Now, for the Biggest Part of the Job

What happens after programmers have untangled the spaghetti code, deleted the dead code, replaced the lost source code, and identified and rewritten every single line of code that refers to a two-digit year?

They've done less than half of the job.

People who've worked on year 2000 projects report that once software has been reprogrammed for Y2K compliance, it must be tested, and that this effort is actually more work than finding and fixing the problem itself. "Depending on the computer language being used, testing could be anywhere from 65 to 70 percent of the job," notes Achi Racov, chief information technology officer for NatWest Group in London.[2]

This testing stage is the most labor-intensive part of the project, and the one for which there are the fewest automated software tools. It's one reason many companies are sending a lot of their year 2000 work to programmers in places such as India and Hungary and the Philippines, usually via a vendor who oversees the work and acts as a middleman. It's not just that there are programmers in these countries willing to work for lower wages, it's that there simply aren't enough programmers in the United States to do the job.

The only thing worse than a huge, tedious, labor-intensive job with an immovable deadline is a huge, tedious, labor-intensive job with an immovable deadline and a shortage of people skilled to do the work. Unfortunately, this is the case with Y2K. The Information Technology Association of America has long noted that hundreds of thousands of high-tech jobs remain unfilled, and the shortage of technology workers is hampering the growth of many American businesses. Bad as the programmer shortage is in general, it's markedly worse when it comes to the year 2000 problem. (For a detailed discussion of why this is, see Chapter Seven.)

Y2K is a major software overhaul that nearly every organization in the world must undertake—and they're all doing it at the same time. It's easy to see why this situation would create an excessive demand for programmers, one the programmers themselves can easily recognize as a temporary opportunity that they should take advantage of while they can.

Many of them are doing just that. Stories abound within the industry of year 2000 experts who can triple their salaries by jumping jobs, and one ex-programmer told me recently he was offered thousands of dollars an hour to work on the year 2000 problem in COBOL/CICS, a particularly sought-after language.

How businesses can cope with all this is also discussed in Chapter Seven. But for now, keep two facts in mind when assessing how hard it is to solve the year 2000 problem:

1. Year 2000 reprogramming requires a living, breathing programmer. The right software tools might speed the process along, but no computer can complete the job on its own.

2. There's a worldwide shortage of programmers who can do the job. The shortage will only get worse as more and more companies wake up to the severity of Y2K.

Last, consider the interconnected nature of today's computers. Few computers operate in a vacuum. Just as the world's businesses are becoming more networked and interdependent, so are the world's computers. Massive amounts of information, much of it containing dates, is passed among them each day.

So even a company that has managed the difficult task of converting all its own software to use four-digit years still faces trouble in the entirely likely event that its computers receive data from outside that use two-digit year fields.

This is why the year 2000 problem is sometimes called the "millennium virus." As with any computer virus, there's a risk of contamination every time your computer accepts data from an external source.

On Time? An Unimpressive Record

Your IT department sets up your new equipment or software, within budget and right on schedule. You flip the switch, start the program, and everything works perfectly. No one using the new system has any trouble at all making it work.

Well, if this rosy description applies to your experience, then your company is highly unusual—and very, very lucky. For most information technology projects, the norm is quite different.

Computer industry experts routinely report that technology projects are finished on schedule less than 20 percent of the time.

Indeed, according to one estimate, at least 96 percent of the time, computer people either deliver a project late or cut back on the scope of the project to get it in on time.

Does this mean computer people are lazy, dishonest, or incapable of proper time management? Not at all. It has to do with the nature of computers and computer programs themselves. Something unexpected almost always goes wrong, and it's practically impossible to predict when it will go right.

When I took my one-and-only programming course in college, I always finished my assignments twenty-four hours before they were due, sometimes staying up half the night to get them done. Not that I was seeking to punish myself or experiment with sleep deprivation; it's just that I could never actually predict when I would be *finished* with a program until the moment, the umpteenth try, when I popped it into the computer and—surprise!—it executed correctly. So, rather than risk being late, I'd actually get things done with a day to spare. I was one of the few who did well in that class, but my other grades suffered because of it. In short, the only way to guarantee even a simple programming project would meet its deadline was to drop everything else and leave lots of extra time.

Life is not much different for today's information technology folks, except that they don't have scholastic vacations in which to recover from staying up all night, or other classes to ignore while they work on software.

"As IT people, we're a very honest group when dealing with other people, but we do have a tendency to lie to ourselves about our ability to deliver," Ulrich said at a recent conference. "We've all worked with people who would gladly work till four in the morning to make a deadline. And a lot of people will be working till four in the morning on a regular basis to address this issue. But at some point you burn out, and you can't continue working those hours."

The Year 2000 Is Sooner Than You Think

If you've been keeping track of year 2000 advice from software experts, then you already know that most of them have advised companies to have all their year 2000 reprogramming finished by January 1, 1999—not December 31, 1999. Why the rush? For two good reasons. The first is that even after your year 2000 solution has been carefully assessed, implemented, and tested, it will almost certainly still contain some bugs.

Bugs are pretty much inevitable in new or upgraded software. This fact is so widely recognized by the computer industry that software developers routinely distribute "beta test" copies of new or upgraded software to thousands of selected users months before releasing it to the general public. Computer experts commonly avoid buying the first version of any new software since they know for a certainty that it is buggy.

The second reason for the recommendation is more crucial. The year 2000 is not waiting until December 31, 1999, to start causing trouble. It's doing that already. Nineteen ninety-nine will see those malfunctions grow exponentially.

The message is clear. If, at this reading, you have not already fixed all your computer systems to account for the year 2000 problem, be prepared for the possibility of severe malfunctions. Prepare for it even if your company's year 2000 project is right on schedule, with a planned completion date sometime between now and January 1, 2000. Chances are that by the time this book comes out, most companies of any size will have seen some systems fail—and malfunctions are going to multiply exponentially during the coming year.

Why will 1999 be so bad? Two reasons. The first is that a malfunction can occur any time a computer encounters a date set in the year 2000. Since many computer programs calculate in one-year increments, they are starting to encounter the year 2000 now.

The second reason has to do with a programming tradition that assigns special meaning to the number 99. It is usually an "end of file" marker telling the program to stop whatever it's doing. "You see, the same programmers, designers, and developers who didn't think their systems would still be in use in the year 2000 also did not believe those same systems would still be in use in the year 1999," explains Y2K consultant Warren S. Reid in an article on his Web page (see Recommended Other Reading).

In fact, here are a few dates during 1999 when it is prudent to plan for widespread malfunctions:

> *April 1.* Not because it's April Fool's Day, but because April is the beginning of the new fiscal year in many organizations. Thus, this date is the beginning of fiscal 2000.

August 22. This date is not worrisome because of the year 2000 problem, but because of what could be seen as its first cousin: a rollover of the Global Positioning System. The GPS is a set of satellites maintained by the U.S. Navy to provide navigational information to ships and planes around the world. It is also used by banks, telecommunications companies, and a host of other systems that require synchronization. All of them may be hopelessly confused when the system resets itself to zero on this date. (Potential GPS problems are described in more detail in Chapter Thirteen.)

September 9. In other words, "9/9/99." Since some systems are programmed to understand a series of 9s as an end-of-file marker, they may all malfunction simultaneously on this day.

And That's Not All

Gruesome as the year 2000 computer problem is, *it may not be the worst part of the year 2000 problem!* Although Y2K affects millions of computers around the world, it also affects many millions more devices that are not computers but contain computer chips. These "embedded" chips are inside pretty much everything with any electronic controls, from a VCR to an airplane to various types of medical equipment. Some of them are in literal terms very deeply embedded, in oil rig equipment sunk into the floor of the ocean, or in thick and indestructible bank vault doors. Unfortunately, they also exist inside what some software experts call "core infrastructure services," such as electric plants, trains, ships, and PBX (multiline telephone) systems.

If the list seems endless, that's because essentially it is. An estimated 25 billion embedded chips are going to be in use around the world by January 1, 2000. The Gartner Group expects about 2 percent of them to malfunction when they encounter the year 2000. That's a small percentage, but a large number of chips—five hundred million. Unlike a computer, an embedded chip cannot be reprogrammed; if a chip is suspect and the device it controls is one that cannot be allowed to fail, then the only alternatives are to replace the chip, or (more probably) the entire device.

Some observers who—despite everything I've detailed so far—are still convinced that the year 2000 software problem is manageable don't feel half so confident about the embedded chip problem. This, they say, is the real cause for concern.

Whether that's true or not, this much is clear: Anyone who thinks the year 2000 problem is easy to fix, or that it can be completely fixed before it causes serious malfunctions, is due for a rude awakening. There are two things every smart business person should be doing. The first is to enlist all available resources in the year 2000 effort at your organization, if you haven't already done so. The second is to recognize that, despite your best efforts, many systems will fail, within your company and in the world at large. Your best hope is to be as prepared for these failures as you can.

Notes

1. Minda Zetlin, "Countdown to Trouble," *Management Review*, American Management Association (May 1997).
2. Ibid.

CHAPTER 3

How Bad Will Things Get?

"By the middle of 2000, New York City will look like Beirut."

—PAUL MILNE, FORMER COMMODITIES BROKER AND YEAR 2000 SURVIVALIST

It's early in January 2000. There's no food in the refrigerator, but you're not sure you can get to the local grocery. None of the traffic lights in town are working. In fact, your electricity has been flickering on and off all day, so that even if you can get food, you're not sure it will keep in your refrigerator.

When you finally do trudge out to the market, you find the shelves surprisingly bare. People have been frantically buying food, and none of the expected shipments have arrived. Still, you collect a few canned goods, bring them to the cash register, and present your credit card—which, of course, is rejected. Disheartened, you trudge home again.

In the last twenty-four hours, stock markets around the world have taken a steep plunge. Most flights and trains into and out of town have been canceled. An angry crowd has gathered on the mall in Washington, worried and enraged over their missing welfare checks. But you don't know about any of this; even when the power is on, your television and radio don't seem to be receiving anything.

As dusk falls, you hear the sound of a mob outside, shouting, running, breaking windows. Frightened, you pick up the phone to dial 911. But of course, there's no dial tone.

A worst-case scenario? Absolutely. Can we be certain that any of this won't happen? Absolutely not. Every event I've described is a plausible result of the year 2000 problem.

This leaves you, the reader, and also me, with something of a dilemma: Just how much chaos should we all be preparing for? Earlier this evening, after I'd spent a few hours working on this chapter and discussed it with my partner (a sophisticated computer professional, by the way), we found ourselves considering such things as solar panels and generators, putting together a stock of nonperishable foods, and even purchasing a shotgun.

The shotgun would be for hunting local game (there are deer and wild turkey in the woods around us) in case of food supply problems. But it could also offer some measure of protection on the off chance that the doommongers are right and there really is widespread societal breakdown. We already live in the country, which some pessimists believe will be safer than the city; we have a wood stove, a vegetable garden, and our own well, though we talked about getting a hand pump for it, in case of extended brownouts.

I wish I could say for certain that we were being paranoid. In some ways, I even wish I could say for certain that we *weren't* being paranoid: at least then I could offer you a concrete plan of action—one that I would be following myself. At this writing, in mid-1998, it seems fairly certain that there will be some disruptions. Exactly how bad they'll be and what shape they'll take is a question to which no one has a sure answer.

"Y2K Born"

Some people are taking no chances. Across the country, groups of "Y2K survivalists" are banding together to create small communities of people who plan to live and work together, safe from whatever year 2000 catastrophes may be affecting the rest of the world. A few extreme doomsayers, who believe that the millennium glitch will ultimately destroy all technology, are actually studying nineteenth-century farming techniques. (Apparently, plowing with a horse is a lot harder than it looks.)

One millennial survivalist, Candace Turner, recently described to the online magazine *Salon* how she first became aware of the millennium bug—an enlightenment she refers to as becoming "Y2K born." Turner, who formerly sold freezers and now sells survival domes—insulated dwellings heated by wood stoves—has also started an online mailing list where she can exchange information and hope with "farmers and others who were Y2K born earlier than I." (For more on this, see www.salon1999.com.)

Think this sounds quasi-religious? I agree. There's no question that for people who've been predicting some sort of millennial apocalypse, Y2K seems made to order.

It's also made to order for those who believe in government conspiracies and a cataclysmic future. For instance, historian Gary North, who has an eighteen-hundred-document Website (see www.garynorth.com) devoted to the coming year 2000 apocalypse, believes that a likely sixty-day shutdown of electric power is enough to end Western civilization. He also believes martial law will be declared by mid-January 2000. Others claim that the U.S. Marines are already quietly being trained to control the population when millennial chaos begins.

Nuclear Fears?

By far the most terrifying possibility to be raised in connection with the year 2000 problem is that of a nuclear accident: a malfunctioning computer, in the United States or elsewhere, glitching and setting off a nuclear weapon.

How probable is something like this? Very, very unlikely, John Pike of the Federation of American Scientists explained to CNN on June 14, 1998—but not absolutely impossible:

> The fundamental problem is that we don't know. Probably nothing's going to happen. [The weapons are] probably just going to sit there and tell their operators: I'm confused. There's a real risk, though, that we could see the sort of computer malfunctions that we've seen in previous years, where the command-and-control systems erroneously report that an attack is in progress. So,

> in all probability, nothing is going to happen, but there is a small, finite risk that this could lead to an accidental nuclear war, simply because people fail to fix their computers. And that's obviously a totally unacceptable risk.

Pike recommends an independent Y2K audit of nuclear arms command-and-control systems, both in the United States and in other countries with nuclear capabilities. This seems like excellent advice to me; similar audits are being effectively conducted in corporations around the globe. But so far, the White House has not been forthcoming when addressed with specific questions about year 2000 compliance in these systems.

Meanwhile, the Defense Department offers assurances that its own nuclear computers won't start any trouble but expresses concern about their Russian counterparts—and offers to share sensitive information about these computers with the Russians in order to avert any possibility of disaster.

Runaway weapons systems are scary enough, but there's a second cause for nuclear concern: the 108 nuclear power plants operated by utility companies around the country, and the hundreds more elsewhere in the world. According to Ed Yourdon, none of these are year 2000-ready at this writing, and it seems unlikely that they all will be before the year 2000 arrives.

Unlike missiles and other weapons, nuclear reactors are designed not to create nuclear destruction under any circumstances, so the chances of the millennium glitch causing an explosion or meltdown seem to be even smaller than those of Y2K-induced nuclear attack. The much greater risk is that reactors could turn themselves off as a result of Y2K, thus interrupting the commercial power supply. If this happens on a widespread basis, it constitutes a catastrophe in its own right.

There's also a risk that the Nuclear Regulatory Commission may force them to shut down. (More on these issues in Chapter Thirteen.)

Since other countries are lagging behind the United States in all aspects of Y2K repair, whatever risk there is of a year 2000-related accident at a power plant is probably greatest abroad. I was particularly dismayed by the Russian Atomic Energy Ministry's recent statement that it is not doing anything to address the year

2000 problem. "We don't have any problems yet," spokesman Vladislav Petrov told the Associated Press. "We'll deal with any problems in the year 2000."[1]

My guess is that the Russian Atomic Energy Ministry, and other nuclear watchdogs around the world, will be goaded out of this if-it-ain't-broke-don't-fix-it attitude by international pressure before the century rollover arrives. As I noted earlier, it's much more likely that a reactor will shut down rather than melt down if it encounters a year 2000 malfunction. But I certainly would feel safer if the Russians were taking the problem a little more seriously. Wouldn't you?

Those in the Know Abandon Ship

If some survivalists, utopians, and others with nonmainstream views have latched onto Y2K as the embodiment of their fears, it's sobering to note that by far the most concerned members of the population seem to be those best able to make an informed judgment: programmers themselves.

It seems frighteningly likely that, just as the worldwide shortage of programmers and engineers threatens the success of Y2K fixes everywhere, these very workers will compound the problem by abandoning cities—and their jobs—"like rats from a sinking ship," as one doommonger put it."

Heritage Farms 2000, the best-known of the Y2K communities, was planned by its founder Russ Voorhees as a "safe haven" in remote South Dakota (where part of the nation's food supply comes from) with satellite links, fiber optics, and solar power that should make it possible for residents to stay connected to the Internet (which will hopefully survive Y2K). Perhaps not surprisingly, the majority of inquiries about the site's five hundred spaces have come from programmers, engineers, and other technology workers.

Yourdon's Epiphany

Of course, the most visible—and most credible—predictor of doom is Ed Yourdon, whose book asks readers to at least consider the possibility of having to survive without such essentials as electricity, phone service, or medicine and food for a period of up to ten years.

Yourdon, who has some thirty years' experience as a software engineering consultant, has published twenty-five books (all of them, until *Time Bomb 2000,* written for IT professionals). He also has his own imprint at Prentice-Hall, has created engineering methodologies in use at thousands of companies, and is generally revered as a programming expert. He first became seriously concerned about two years ago, as he realized that many of the corporate Y2K projects he was reviewing were doomed to failure. Nothing unusual about hopeless projects, he adds—he's seen many in his day. "You know they're doomed—they won't admit it, they may not even know it, but it's obvious. And I'd say, well, that's OK, I'll collect my consulting fee, and I'll make sure that I'm not standing anywhere near this thing when it goes under." (For more on this see www.salon1999.com.)

But Y2K, he realized, was different. "Because it's everything—it's every insurance company and every utility company. And if they all go down, and they're all interconnected, then my family goes down with it." That realization, he says now, was something of an epiphany.

What frightens Yourdon, and many other predictors of Y2K doom, is the interdependence of computer systems, industries, governments, and utilities, such that one serious malfunction can send shock waves in unexpected directions.

One object lesson in how this works was the 1997 United Parcel Service strike, which lasted only sixteen days but threatened the survival of many small mail-order businesses that suddenly found themselves unable to get products into customers' hands. It's easy to imagine how many of these businesses—and other types of enterprise as well—might be forced to close their doors if there were a prolonged interruption in any one of many services whose absolute solidity we have all come to take for granted.

"If any component of the iron triangle (banking, telecommunications, and electricity) fails in a Year-2000 collapse, the other two are likely to fail quickly too," Yourdon writes. "And if the iron triangle goes down, most of what we refer to as 'modern society' goes down with it."

Yourdon has, as it were, put his Y2K money where his mouth is. He has gotten out of the stock market, and at this writing, he and his family are in the process of moving from Manhattan to a home in New Mexico, which, he believes, will be safer when the Y2K storm breaks. None of these decisions, he says, were easy to make, any more than the recommendations in his book are painless for readers to follow. But, he stresses, it's important to make them now, while there's still a little time to maneuver.

A Reasonable Course?

Given that Yourdon is a well-known, highly respected, and eminently reasonable man who is taking this issue very seriously to heart, it's difficult to dismiss his warnings as overblown. On the other hand, making preparations to get along for a month or more without, say, electricity or groceries is simply more than most people are willing to undertake, at least as I write this in mid-1998. Some who *are* willing won't be able to do what he advises, most of which demands geographical flexibility, free time, storage space, and, in particular, available funds.

Short of signing up for Heritage Farms 2000 (which I suspect will be full by the time this book is published anyway), what can a reasonable person do to prepare for Y2K? Is there a middle course between going blindly into the unknown with no preparations made and cleaning out your savings account to buy one of Turner's geodesic domes?

I believe there is, though of course there is no guarantee.

Plan for Less-Than-Complete Chaos

Some of the direst year 2000 prognosticators think the glitch will bring about the fall of the U.S. Government, among other things rendering the dollar worthless. Thus they advise purchasing gold as a more dependable currency. Does that sound extreme to you? It does to me, too. Likewise, I think a month with no electricity at all is both highly unlikely and more or less impossible to prepare for. (On the other hand, in my opinion a month's worth of power rationing and brown-outs is easier to anticipate and worth preparing for.)

In general, I think it's more doable, and probably more realistic, to assume that at least some of our governmental and utility infrastructure will remain in place. Plan for short interruptions and major hassles, but not total anarchy.

Be as Flexible as Possible

Y2K is an unknown, and the best way to plan for an unknown is to retain as much flexibility as you can. For both individuals and businesses, I think the first step toward flexibility should be to preserve liquidity; this is not the time to mortgage yourself up to the eyeballs. (An opposing viewpoint is that if banking institutions are about to lose all their records, now would be a great time to take out a large loan—in the hope that your debit vanishes without a trace. Personally, I think this is wishful thinking, and unacceptably risky.)

This may likewise not be the time for a major property purchase, not only because doing so ties up cash and reduces flexibility but also because Y2K will inevitably have some deleterious effect on the economy, and, thus, property values.

Some questions of flexibility are more complex—and deeper. One example: My partner and I have been discussing the possibility of having a child. This has raised a whole host of conflicting desires and priorities and is most emphatically not a question that will be settled by Y2K. But some of the possible scenarios are just disturbing enough to make me wonder if it would be wise to give birth, or care for a newborn, during the worst of the disruptions.

Learn as Much as You Can

A little knowledge is a very useful thing. The most important thing to do about the year 2000 problem is understand it. Then stay informed about it; information about this issue is becoming clearer by the day. When I worked on the briefing version of this book a year ago, it was possible to guess that there might be severe disruptions, but not necessarily of what sort. Now, it's become a lot easier to make informed judgments. For instance, it now seems clear that the element of the iron triangle most in danger of serious trouble is electric power.

If you're not willing to make the most difficult preparations right now, your next best course is to keep close tabs on the situation and be ready to move quickly if you believe action is warranted. The Cap Gemini surveys I mentioned in the Introduction make it clear that a substantial number of companies have already had year 2000 malfunctions. Still, there have been very few publicly obvious ones, mostly having to do with two-digit expiration dates on goods or credit cards.

By the time this book appears, things will probably change. For the reasons discussed in Chapter Two, it's likely that early 1999 will see a growing crop of Y2K malfunctions. What this means is that someone reading this book in early 1999 can get a much better idea than I can have right now as to just how bad year 2000 disruptions are likely to be.

Carefully observing the nature of these malfunctions, how they're dealt with, and how much trouble they cause should give you an idea of what type of disruptions to expect at the end of 1999 and how severe these may be. If they're small disruptions that are easily and efficiently dealt with, then we can hope that the disruptions we see in January 2000 will be more or less manageable. If there are severe disruptions, the outlook may be much grimmer. (On the plus side, a spate of highly visible disruptions early in 1999 might have the useful effect of elevating Y2K to the top of everyone's priority list.)

Even if we do get through early 1999 without too much trouble, though, it doesn't mean we're home free. Keep in mind that the millennium glitch hits only *some* computers then. It doesn't tell us anything about possible problems with embedded chips, most of which won't try to process year 2000 dates until the actual year 2000 arrives.

Get It in Writing—If You Can

As much as possible, try to spread your year 2000 risk. If you haven't yet done so, look into your insurance status to see if you are covered for any Y2K mishaps. Ask for written guarantees that the products you lease, or are about to buy, are year 2000-ready. At a minimum, this should apply to any new computer hardware, software, and electronic equipment, but it should also apply to some things we don't normally think of as computerized, such as security doors.

Unfortunately, these written guarantees are difficult to come by and are getting more so all the time.

Getting things in writing also means keeping a complete "paper trail" of every transaction you make from now at least until the summer of 2000. Some of the snafus I presented in the opening pages of this book serve to illustrate how easily Y2K can make such things as accounts disappear, and your ability to show that you've already paid your bill—or perhaps even demonstrate that you exist—may depend on having written proof of what you've done in the past.

Stockpile a Little

Experts agree that late 1999 is no time for just-in-time inventory techniques. By the same token, you should probably have some extra supplies of nonperishable foods, paper products, and bottled water, enough to last a few days in case of supply or travel disruptions. You should have a longer-term supply of any medicines you depend on, because medicines (most of which are made from components that have been shipped from overseas) may be in short supply if the year 2000 glitch has a severe impact on transportation. This kind of precaution is so easy and obvious that it's foolish *not* to do so.

Should you take your money out of the bank and hide it under your mattress (or in some other safe hiding place)? I would say definitely not. The banking industry has been ahead of most others in its year 2000 repairs, partly because Y2K is a top priority of the Federal Deposit Insurance Corporation—which, by the way, insures deposits of up to $100,000. Given these facts, it seems to me that bank deposits are safe enough.

A more practical question is whether you should have some extra cash on hand, say enough to get through a couple of weeks. Here again, I believe most ATMs will keep working, but some may glitch for a while, and for people like me who live fairly far away from their bank, getting to the ATM might prove difficult. A few months ago, the Federal Reserve began considering what might happen if a major portion of the nation's population sought to have an unusually large amount of cash at the same time; as a result, the Fed has decided to print extra currency in preparation for New Year's 2000. As long as they're printing it, we might as well go ahead and withdraw it.

Plan Short-Term Alternatives to Basic Services

As I've said, if such things as water, electricity, and telecommunications all vanish for an entire month, the world we live in will become so unrecognizable that many of our basic assumptions will turn out to be false, and many of our preparations are likely to prove worthless.

But there may be short-term disruptions, and you can prepare for them with such things as candles, oil lamps, kerosene heaters (remember that New Year's Day comes in the dead of winter), and backup generators. If you're highly dependent on public transportation, consider making a carpool contingency plan, for instance. This is something that can and should be done at a company level, to ensure that the highest possible percentage of employees can get to work if there are delays. An alternative might be to make plans for some people to be able to work at home, if necessary.

Those of us who live in rural areas, especially areas where there are severe snowstorms, are already quite accustomed to having occasional periods when our power, phones, and usual sources of heat aren't operating. We know it's simple enough to cope for a few days without these services, and extremely difficult to deal with longer outages than that. Being prepared to deal with a short disruption already puts you ahead of the game.

Limit Your Dependence on Overseas Suppliers

Sadly, the United States leads every other country on earth in its preparations for the year 2000. Many other countries are certain to be caught off guard when the millennium bug strikes. (For a more detailed look at the international picture, see Chapter Fourteen.)

Given the likelihood of problems overseas and in the shipping industry, it's just not smart to be completely dependent on anything that must be imported. Prudence suggests that you at least prepare a backup source, just in case.

A Word About Computer Dependence

As I've talked to people about the year 2000 problem over the past several months, I've encountered a certain type of reaction from many people who have never felt comfortable with computer technology and now feel that every fear they've ever had is justified. "Aha!" they say. "We always knew typewriters were better than word processors! Typewriters couldn't be laid low by something so simple as a two-digit year. We were right all along: Computers are completely undependable, and all the people who ever trusted them are only getting what they deserve!"

An understandable point of view, but I believe the opposite is true. The year 2000 problem, in a roundabout way, is proving how dependable computers have always been. If computers really were as untrustworthy as these people believe, then we wouldn't have been counting on so many of them all these years to do everything from flying airplanes to keeping nuclear reactors running safely, to monitoring pacemakers, to controlling the atomic weapons my generation grew up fretting about.

The fact that computers in general have been so utterly dependable for so many years is the very reason why Y2K is now so frightening.

Note

1. "Agency Waits to Fix Computer Bug," Associated Press (June 19, 1998).

CHAPTER 4

How Could They Let This Happen?

"It would be just like programmers to shorten the year 2000 problem to Y2K—exactly the kind of thinking that created this situation in the first place!"

—SOURCE UNKNOWN

If you're grappling with the year 2000 problem, facing massive disruptions in goods and services, and contemplating spending huge sums on a project whose only benefit is that you can continue operating as before, you're probably having a very natural reaction: You're mad as hell and looking for someone to blame.

It looks as if there *is* someone to blame: those nameless, faceless programmers who created the two-digit year field in the early days of computing. Didn't they know the millennium was coming?

Why Did They Do This to Us?

It's very tempting to blame the programming community for the year 2000 problem, but that's neither accurate nor fair. Programmers created the millennium glitch for three very good reasons:

1. It seemed like a good idea at the time. In fact, given the information available when most programs were written, it *was* a good idea at the time.

2. Once the year 2000 problem was in place, it became self-perpetuating.
3. A few farsighted programmers did try to avoid Y2K—and were promptly overruled by their bosses.

It Seemed Like a Good Idea at the Time

For those of us who've accepted the World Wide Web as a fact of daily life, it can be difficult to remember how dramatically computers have changed in a remarkably short time.

But they have. Twenty years ago, when this industry was in its infancy, programmers still entered data into computers on hole punch cards, each with eighty columns of characters. Even computers that had evolved to use keyboards for data entry often operated on "virtual cards" using the same eighty-column format.

Whether one was using keyboards or cards, one thing remained constant: Memory storage space was precious, both monetarily and as a corporate resource. One megabyte of storage cost more than $2,000 a year in 1963, and more than $400 in 1972. It costs about a dollar today. (Please note that what I am referring to here is memory storage, in disk or tape form, not the megabytes of random access memory, or RAM, many personal computer users are adding to make their machines function more powerfully.)

Surprisingly, what this means is that the programming practices that created Y2K actually showed sound business judgment. In an article in the inaugural issue of the *Year/2000 Journal* (see Recommended Other Reading), year 2000 experts Leon Kappelman and Phil Scott estimate that, for an average company, about 3 to 6 percent of stored data are dates. Using eight digits instead of six would have meant an increase in storage space of 33 percent for those items. Even assuming that only 3 percent of a company's data are dates, that amounts to a savings of 1 percent; but because memory used to be so expensive, 1 percent represented a huge saving. In one case, the authors note, a company that estimated it would need a modest ten gigabytes of average storage from 1963 to 1992 figured it saved at least $100 million in current dollars—and perhaps as much as $1 billion.

In light of this, the authors argue that given the billions that have been saved over the past thirty-five years by using six rather than eight digits to store dates, the practice that created the year 2000 problem showed wise business judgment even with 20-20 hindsight. Even the billions now needed to solve the problem are a smaller sum than what use of six-digit dates saved.

It Became Self-Perpetuating

Once the year 2000 problem was in place, it was self-perpetuating.

Given the terrible risks the entire world is running if Y2K isn't solved in time, I'm hesitant to agree that using two-digit years was ever a worthwhile bargain, no matter how many millions were saved. But programmers of old had another seemingly good reason not to worry about the year 2000: They figured that the computers and programs we would be using when the new millennium arrived would be unrecognizably different from what we had back then. One programmer told me he was told to assume any software he created needed to be valid for seven to ten years, after which it would be replaced. Of course, by today's standards, that's a ridiculously long time; most computer users wouldn't be caught dead with seven-year-old software. At this writing, Windows 95 is less than three years old but already rendered obsolete by Windows 98.

What no one understood was *how* software would evolve, always building on past work rather than starting fresh. Countless older "legacy" systems have been upgraded, reconfigured, and refurbished again and again, without ever actually being replaced. Likewise, rather than reinventing the wheel every time they sit down to write a piece of software, programmers typically build on existing material.

What this means is that at least as recently as 1998, programs were being written that were not year 2000-compliant. I found this hard to believe when I first heard about it. I was so astounded that I posted a question about it on an online computer programming message board. One COBOL programmer wrote back, "I must admit, I just completed a major development effort in which we set a four-digit year standard for the code in the application, and some two-digit year code still slipped through, specifically related to calendar quarter designations."

He added, perhaps unnecessarily: "Rigid quality assurance review in this area is needed for programs being written today."

It's not that programmers are lazy or careless. But modern programs have so many hundreds of thousands of lines of code in them that to create each one from scratch would be hopelessly inefficient and prohibitively expensive. So they really have no choice but to lift sections of software from existing programs, some of which are not year 2000-compliant.

Careful programmers may catch some of these errors, but they don't always. Thus, unfortunately, it's extremely common for organizations to find themselves installing newly developed software that is not year 2000-compliant. Often these are complex, powerful programs that took months or even years to create.

What this means for your company is that solving the year 2000 problem may be something like painting the Golden Gate Bridge: By the time you get to the end you have to start at the beginning again. Although painting the bridge may make sense as a permanently ongoing project, your year 2000 conversion project is something you have to finish or else risk real consequences to your organization.

There's only one way to stop this vicious cycle: Make sure every new or upgraded piece of software is subjected to stringent year 2000 testing before allowing it to be installed on your company's computers. Unfortunately, you need to apply this rule not only to software you've developed in house or had custom-written for you, but also to software you've received from vendors—even if that software is supposed to be Y2K-free.

"We got some software that our vendor had certified as compliant," noted David Kelble, project manager for Wawa, a chain of Pennsylvania dairies and food markets at an American Management Association (AMA) conference. "We gave it to our year 2000 consultant, and he broke it in about ten minutes! By "broke it," Kelble means that the consultant was able to identify a year 2000 malfunction. His story is not unusual. I've heard similar tales from many other Y2K project managers. It's even true of some shrink-wrapped PC-based software on the shelves of stores today.

It's not that the vendors mean to be dishonest. It's just that their programmers, too, have to reuse existing code. Not only that, it's extremely difficult to devise a test that accounts for every possible combination of functions with every possible date. This is one reason some year 2000 consultants are now using the term *year 2000-ready* instead of *year 2000-compliant*—because they believe full compliance is an impossible goal.

Programmers Were Overruled by Their Bosses

Not all programmers have been as shortsighted as you may think. Believe it or not, some veteran programmers who sent in comments that were used in Morgan Stanley's special report on Y2K (see Recommended Reading) reported that they tried to bring the year 2000 problem to their bosses' attention way back in the dark ages of computing. Tried, and failed.

One of these programmers who was working on a program that tracked birth dates and included a few from the nineteenth century asked out of curiosity what would happen when two-digit years met the turn of the century. The answer was a shrug and a laugh. "I let it go," he says. Other programmers recall their bosses' answer: "We'll all be retired by then!" Ironically, many of those who did retire are now coming back to work on year 2000 projects for salaries beyond their wildest dreams.

Another programmer says: "It was those stupid bean counters, they would never approve the purchase of disk drives. Told us they were too expensive, and to find some other way to keep the computers running." Still another recalls: "I was there in the sixties, and I know how precious resources were. A large disk drive was ten or twenty megabytes—if you had a disk drive. . . . It was tough getting things to fit on machines as every byte was precious. Putting '19' in a date could have gotten you fired."

An exaggeration? Probably not. In the current climate of mounting Y2K panic, most top executives are now accepting the year 2000 problem as an emergency they must take steps to fix. Although, surprisingly, even at this writing some year 2000 projects have been vetoed or canceled by managers who are still somehow under the impression that dealing with Y2K is optional.

Just a couple of years ago, that attitude was the rule, not the exception. One IT manager told me—who wishes to remain anonymous—that when he first asked his company's top management for resources to deal with Y2K, he was told it was a computer problem that his department had to handle on its own. He finally got the support he needed—but not until he threatened to quit.

"I said, 'You're telling me this has nothing to do with the business and I have to solve the problem myself?'" he reports. "That's like if the leg had gangrene and the body said, 'You solve the problem, leg. It has nothing to do with me.'" This was in late 1994—and he worked in banking, one of the first industries to recognize the year 2000 problem.

The worst example of this that I've heard concerns "Al," the CIO at a major manufacturing company. Al was one of the visionary few who began thinking about the year 2000 problem ten years ago, when it would have been relatively easy to solve. He realized that the most painless way to fix it would be through attrition—something that would still have been possible back then. As the company's computer systems went through their natural upgrades, each one could be double-checked for year 2000 compliance. By the time the millennium rolled around, the whole company would have its year 2000 problem solved, without enormous hassle or expense.

Al described his concerns about the year 2000 problem, and offered his suggestions for solving it, to his company's top management. They politely told him he was out of his mind. In the mid-1980s, nobody had ever heard of the year 2000 problem. Or if they had, it was the stuff of dinner-party jokes.

Most people who thought about it were all quite certain that way before the deadline came, software vendors would have invented some magical fix to prevent the 00 date from causing trouble. In any case, how could they worry about an uncertain problem ten years into the future when they had serious concerns that demanded immediate attention?

Al kept after them, reminding them of the danger, voicing his concerns at every executive session he attended. Eventually, he became so much of an annoyance that he was fired. At the time, he thought his career had been derailed forever. Today, he runs a successful year 2000 consulting firm. Present-day executives who want to lay the blame for Y2K on the programming profession should keep Al's story in mind.

Expense Rather Than Investment

Not long ago, I heard author and publisher Paul Strassman give a speech at a conference in which he said, "I lay [the year 2000 problem] at the feet of the management of corporate America, which always looked at software as an expense rather than an investment."

The more I think about it, the more it makes sense to me. Many top executives, especially those who have come from a less-technological era, seem to think of both hardware and software as a necessary evil—something you must have because you can't do business without them. Software, in particular, is rarely seen as an asset, even though we're now squarely in the information age and software is actually nothing more than a very complex collection of information.

If you think about it, this assumption that software has no lasting value is implicit in the often-repeated view that solving the year 2000 problem offers no business benefit except the ability to continue doing business as usual. Or, at best, perhaps an edge on the competition, if *we* can keep serving customers as usual while *they* suffer year 2000-related interruptions.

But what if, for one moment, we change this underlying assumption? In that case, solving the year 2000 problem takes on a whole new economic outlook! Especially when you consider all the other problems I've described in detail in Chapter Two, such as spaghetti code and lost source code, which need to be dealt with on the way to solving Y2K. Even if your company can only fix a few systems, those systems will be clearly coded, well documented, and year 2000-ready. If software is an asset, then clearly those assets substantially increase in value.

Geeks Versus Bean Counters?

There's another, even more troubling assumption under the surface here: that IT people and business people are somehow completely separate, living in separate worlds with separate priorities, and cannot possibly share the same goals. Computer people are "techies" or "geeks," known to enjoy working all night in front of computer screens while munching pizza, and to have limited social lives. Dilbert, in other words. Whereas the techies think of business people as "bean counters" (recall the blaming comment from a programmer) or "users" (as in computer users) or "the business side." Dilbert's pointy-haired boss, in other words.

What's most troubling about this is the unstated view that the two disciplines must always have completely divergent goals. The business people have no interest in technology. They want user-friendly computers so they can use them without bothering to understand them. They see technology as nothing more than a means to an end, a tool that—at best—can help them achieve some business goals. The technology people, on the other hand, are motivated only by their love of technology. The only way to incentivize them is to offer them the newest, coolest, most up-to-the-minute technology to play with.

In fact, IT people in general have been accused of keeping Y2K secret for exactly this reason: The funds and resources needed to deal with the year 2000 problem would preclude the exciting new technology projects they dream of. (As Peter de Jager put it at a recent conference, "You can't have any new toys until you clean up your room!")

There's certainly no denying that the programming community at large has been aware of the year 2000 problem for many more years than the rest of us yet somehow failed to pass that awareness along. It's striking to remember how many IT managers, who certainly should have known better, downplayed Y2K as an easily solved problem in 1994, 1995, and even 1996. If the accusation is true, then it bears thinking about for a minute. It means that IT people were willing to put the very survival of their own companies at risk, rather than give up pet technology projects. It's hard to imagine priorities less in line with those of "the business side."

On the other hand, this strategy might make a lot of sense, from an IT person's point of view. Remember that years of layoffs and downsizing have taught employees not to expect job security, but rather to think of the job as an opportunity to better their skills and thus be more attractive to prospective employers. In other words, staying current with new technology is a better guarantee of a good future than keeping one's employer in business. If employees have come to see their companies this way, top managers have no one but themselves to blame.

But there's another possibility we should remember: IT people may have kept mum about the year 2000 problem out of plain, old-fashioned fear. "People are afraid to talk to senior management," notes Lauris Nance, assistant vice president and year 2000 project manager for Equifax. "It's real tough to go in and tell somebody that you have a major project, it's going to cost a considerable amount, you didn't budget it, and you didn't plan for it. If you have the option of not giving that bad news, you usually don't. People love to shoot the messenger."[1]

Whether the IT community kept Y2K under wraps out of fear or a greedy desire for new technology, the fact that business leaders didn't properly understand this issue until it was too late tells us that something is drastically wrong with how technology people and business people have been working together so far. I dislike the term *paradigm shift*, but it seems to me that one is needed here because, clearly, as we enter the twenty-first century, proper management of technology is a make-or-break issue for many companies.

In this respect, the year 2000 problem may actually be a help. This is too big a project for the techies to handle alone, and at the same time too big a problem for business people to ignore. In the end, they may have no choice but to learn to communicate more clearly and work more effectively together. If so, it will be Y2K's biggest benefit of all.

Note

1. Minda Zetlin, "Countdown to Trouble," *Management Review*, American Management Association (May 1997).

CHAPTER 5

The Second Costliest Problem in History

"It is an interesting 'sanity check' to see how the year 2000 costs relate to the overall cost per capita for U.S. citizens. Assuming a year 2000 population for the United States of about 280 million citizens, then the per capita year 2000 cost for the United States amounts to about $989 for every citizen. Assuming a U.S. working population at the end of the century of roughly 120 million workers, then about $2,308 would be the cost for every working person in the United States."

—CAPERS JONES

As Jones's comment shows,[1] discussions of the overall worldwide cost for fixing the year 2000 problem always take on a somewhat surreal quality because the numbers involved are unimaginably huge. Projections range from $300 billion, the low end of the Gartner Group's range, to a Giga Information Group estimate of more than $3 *trillion*. To put these staggering figures into more human perspective, the year 2000 will be the second most expensive event ever to face humanity—the first being World War II, which (adjusted for inflation) cost more than $4 trillion. All other human wars and disasters have been less expensive, although the Vietnam war, at an estimated $500 billion, comes close.

Please note that the high estimate just above is about ten times bigger than the low estimate! Nothing, in my opinion, could better illustrate the tremendous uncertainty about how the year 2000 problem will actually play out. In fact, it's impossible to predict exactly how much the year 2000 problem will finally cost when all is said and done. For one thing, expenses for hiring programmers and year 2000 consultants are rising rapidly as the supply of available expertise diminishes, and companies scramble to sign up whomever they can. Furthermore, most organizations and governments still do not have a complete grasp of what changes they need to make to achieve year 2000 compliance—as of this writing an estimated 40 percent still have not formulated a full-fledged year 2000 plan—or how exactly to carry out those changes. The numerous year 2000-related lawsuits already being filed are another wild card (and bound to grow exponentially); no one can predict with any accuracy whatsoever how much all this litigation is likely to cost once the dust settles, hopefully by sometime in 2010. It's worth noting, though, that most early estimates have been revised upward as the year 2000 approaches.

Of course, these estimates don't take into account the very real risk of cataclysmic infrastructure disruptions. If any element of the iron triangle described in Chapter Two goes down, or if shipping, transportation, or manufacturing are badly impaired, or if there is a Y2K-related nuclear disaster (a *very* remote possibility), then of course even the astronomical costs predictions above will be much, much too low.

Whatever the final amount turns out to be, the United States being both the most computerized and the most litigious country on earth, American businesses are sure to spend a disproportionately large share of that money.

A 70 Percent Chance of Recession

Federal Reserve Chairman Alan Greenspan has warned repeatedly that the year 2000 problem and its attendant disruptions and expenses constitute one of the most serious threats to future prosperity. Astoundingly, most economists have so far refused to consider the year 2000 in their forecasts.

With one notable exception. Edward Yardeni, chief economist for Deutsche Bank Securities, has spent a lot of time collecting and analyzing the data available about the year 2000 problem and its likely economic effects. He offers some of these analyses in a "Netbook" and in his publication, *The Y2K Reporter*, both available on the Web (see Recommended Reading).

Yardeni first began studying Y2K's potential effects in the summer of 1997; he concluded that there was a 30 percent chance of global recession, comparable in severity to the recession of 1973–1974, which, he notes, was caused by interruption of the worldwide supply of oil. "Similarly, a disruption in the flow of information caused by the year 2000 problem has the potential to trigger a severe global downturn," he observes.

In November 1997, he raised the odds to 40 percent, based on disappointing reports of the federal government's progress in addressing Y2K. In March 1998, he raised the odds to 60 percent, and in June, as I was at work on this book, he increased them to 70 percent.

The most recent increases were responses to what Yardeni believes are inadequate government responses to the millennium glitch. Despite repeated claims of official confidence, there is no evidence to suggest that the federal government is able to deal with the year 2000 problem in time to avoid disruptions. What little evidence there is tends to suggest the opposite.

If there is to be a recession, Yardeni adds, it might well begin in the last six months of 1999, for any combination of several reasons:

1. An alarmed public will pull funds out of the stock market, triggering a steep decline, which will in turn erode consumer confidence.
2. Banks may refuse credit to companies that are not adequately prepared for Y2K (something they are already beginning to do).
3. As a result, some of these companies may begin failing in 1999.

This possible recession, Yardeni adds, could last as long as a year and trigger a reduction in the Gross Domestic Product of as much as 4 percent (by comparison, it fell by 3.7 percent during the 1973–1974 recession). Yardeni also believes that, unlike the oil crisis of the 1970s, the Y2K recession will not be accompanied by inflation—in fact, it will probably lead to deflation, perhaps of as much as

5 percent. Combined with his anticipated reduction in GDP, this could mean a loss of $1 trillion for the U.S. economy alone.

Further, he notes, the stock market falls in every recession, and the Dow Jones Industrial Average dropped 42 percent in the 1973-1974 period. A similar drop in 1999 or 2000 would bring the Dow from its 1998 high of about 9,000 to about 5,200—and mean a loss of another $1 trillion to U.S. stockholders.

Dr. Yardeni's Prescription

Though Yardeni believes everything described above is more likely to happen than not, he also believes that the worst could be avoided if world governments are persuaded to take the problem seriously, give it top priority, and pull together toward a common solution. With this in mind, he proposes these steps:

1. I would like to see the United States and every country on this planet establish national Y2K War Councils to coordinate the repair efforts and to prepare for the disruptive consequences of inevitable failures domestically and globally.
2. Intra- and interindustry Y2K cooperatives should be established nationally and globally to pool resources, establish standards, and coordinate testing.
3. Organizations that actively and openly cooperate with others should be protected from legal liability as much as possible.
4. We should study whether a one-week worldwide Y2K holiday might be necessary so that the global computer system won't be stress tested under peak load conditions.
5. We should consider stress testing the global computer system a month before January 1, 2000, to determine the weakest links in the global IT chain.
6. The number one priority must be to make sure that the utilities supplying electricity, gas, water, and phone services will all function properly.

7. Also at the top of the priority list are air and rail transportation, banking and finance, and government revenue and payments systems.

8. In the United States, we should increase government spending to buy new computers for every federal, state, and local agency that needs them for the coming century. The federal budget will certainly be in deficit again in a year 2000 recession. Better to be in deficit in 1999 to repair Y2K and to prepare for problems so as to minimize the consequences of such a recession.[2]

Every one of these is a commendable idea, but it seems highly unlikely that most of them can be put into action. In particular, though I'm a strong believer in human nature and basically an optimist, I have a hard time imagining the world coordinating itself enough to put together a rigorous, global test of computer systems by December 1999.

I also can't see Congress allocating anywhere near enough funds to replace governmental computer systems all over the country. Indeed, such replacements take time, and even if all these government agencies received a blank check in tomorrow's mail, I don't believe they could replace their systems in time for the new millennium.

An Unavoidable Downturn

In my opinion, it is unfortunately no longer possible to avoid a serious economic downturn.

With a little luck and a lot of hard work, it may still be possible to prevent massive disruptions in power, transportation, utilities, and finance. I hope and believe that, as the dangers posed by Y2K become more of a reality in the minds of government leaders, some concerted efforts are made to avoid the kind of disasters that have the millennium survivalists preparing their solar panels and shotguns. But even if we get through the century rollover without any serious disruptions, I don't see how the year 2000 problem can fail to affect the world economy.

I've set my online service to flag stories containing the phrase "year 2000" that come over the Associated Press wire.

Every quarter, it seems I get a few in which large companies report lower than expected earnings because of the huge sums they have had to spend on the year 2000 problem. This is at a time when many companies have not yet made a realistic assessment of their year 2000 costs, and most that have done so haven't fully shared the information. (This may be about to change, however, as I suggest later in this chapter.)

Inevitably, there will be an effect on the stock market. In fact, I would argue it is already starting to happen, in the form of both lower earnings and lower productivity. (More about this in Chapter Sixteen.)

Can You Profit From Y2K?

What does all this mean to you and your organization? Certainly, all investment strategies for the next few years should take into account the likelihood of a Y2K-driven economic downturn. Yardeni's recommendation is to head for such investments as treasury bonds, and to avoid stocks in industries such as air travel that are likely to be affected by the glitch. Some investors are also trying to make a buck from Y2K by investing in selected technology companies—which have, so far, proved pretty volatile—and by shorting companies they believe will be affected. There are even a few mutual funds designed to take advantage of the year 2000 problem in this manner.

This kind of investing in the year 2000 seems to me a chancy proposition at best. Investing in industries that are likely to benefit from Y2K (such as temporary clerical help—because nonfunctioning computers may need to be replaced by human helpers) may be slightly more effective.

What isn't possible, at least not as I write this, is to judge a company's vulnerability to the year 2000 problem by studying its financial reports. Right now, most of these statements don't provide enough information for a shareholder to make an informed evaluation. Giga Information Group recently released a survey of one thousand corporate 10K filings, in which it found that only 25 percent mentioned the cost of year 2000 repairs at all, and that even those describing the problem offered too little information.

The Securities and Exchange Commission, however, is rapidly losing patience with these paltry or nonexistent year 2000 disclosures. In January 1998, it asked (nicely) for publicly traded corporations to make their Y2K status known to investors. But as the Giga Group study shows, the SEC didn't get much voluntary cooperation. So in August, SEC chairman Arthur Levitt, Jr., took the unusual step of sending letters to ten thousand CEOs of publicly traded companies, telling them to provide fuller year 2000 information or risk fines. It also sent out fifteen thousand more letters warning of Y2K dangers to brokerage houses and investment advisors. Whether this is enough to pull the fig leaf off corporate year 2000 problems remains to be seen. But at least it's clear that when it comes to the year 2000 problem, the SEC means business.

In addition to tailoring your investment strategy with Y2K in mind, it's also important to keep in mind both the likelihood of economic hard times and the high expense of fixing your company's own year 2000 problem when making spending decisions. Chances are that 1999 is the wrong year to start a new venture that leaves your company cash poor.

More Than You Expected to Spend?

Nearly every company undertaking a year 2000 repair finds itself spending more than originally planned—usually a lot more. "One of our clients came up with about $60 million to solve the problem," recalls Chuck White, a Gartner Group vice president and research director. "The more they looked at it, though, the more the budget kept going up. At this point, they're on their third pass, and the estimate is up to $140 million."[3]

You may be tempted to think that this company is bad at making budget projections, but stories like these are quite common. The reason why is in the nature of the year 2000 problem itself. As one IT executive put it, "Every time you open a door in this project, you find ten more doors behind it."

In the meantime, salaries for programmers and other year 2000 expenses are growing as corporate panic sets in. The message is clear: Whatever you may be planning to spend to solve the year 2000 problem, be prepared to lay out a lot more. Chances are, it will cripple most companies' ability to undertake new technology projects.

You may also be tempted to recoup some of this apparent waste of money by incorporating other elements (such as a general upgrade to more modern software) into your company's year 2000 project. This certainly seems more appealing: If you're going to spend huge sums, why not get some sort of improved technology out of the deal?

Don't do it. This adding of extraneous projects is what programmers call "scope creep," and it can derail your whole effort to get Y2K corrected before malfunctions start to occur. "It was a great idea five years ago," said consultant and author Ian Hayes at a conference recently. "Now, there just isn't time."

Some Cost Guidelines

One piece of information that has emerged from even the barebones SEC filings public companies have already submitted is that many large companies are seriously underestimating their year 2000 expenses. Whatever the size and scope of your year 2000 problem, some rough guidelines may help plan year 2000 costs. Admittedly, these are educated guesses. But taken together, they might help you determine if your budget is in line with reality.

- Experts agree a typical year 2000 effort will cost at least 30 percent of an organization's annual information technology budget.

- Most year 2000 repairs are assumed to cost $1.50 per line of code within a company's software portfolio. Wide variations from this price are possible, but it serves as a fairly good budgeting standard. Of course, it won't do you much good if you don't know how many lines of code you have, and if by the time this book is published you still don't, then it's not going to be worth taking the time to do an inventory to find out.

- It is helpful to note, however, that even a small company may easily have ten million or more lines of code, and large companies may have hundreds of millions.

- There are other costs. This $1.50 per line of code refers only to direct year 2000 repair work. Chances are, your company may also have to pay for:

  - Repairing or replacing personal computers, client server systems, and related software that are not year 2000-compliant
  - Upgrading off-the-shelf software that is not year 2000-compliant
  - Business problems associated with the year 2000 (for instance, you may have to switch suppliers or keep a greater inventory because of potential year 2000 problems at your supplier companies)
  - Interruptions in basic services, such as electricity or phone service
  - Replacing hardware
  - Replacing devices containing embedded chips that may not be year 2000-compliant
  - Extra clerical and staff time as workers take over computer tasks (such as invoicing) that were not corrected in time
  - Special year 2000 insurance

- Our litigious society being what it is, there's a high likelihood you'll be involved somehow in a year 2000 lawsuit. Capers Jones estimates that the cost for this may run from $3 to more than $20 per line of code.

- The more behind you are, the more it will cost. Hiring programmers or vendors to work on your year 2000 problem is getting more difficult, and more expensive, by the day. So, how far along you are or aren't in your repair may be a big part of determining how much the entire effort costs. For instance, if by this time you're still in the assessment or triage phase, expect not only to have system malfunctions but to pay top dollar for year 2000 repairs.

- Mergers can aggravate year 2000 expenses.

At United Healthcare, based in Hartford, Connecticut, a well-organized IT department started its year 2000 project in plenty of time for the new

> millennium. The company determined that it had 120 million lines of code in its inventory. Because the IT department got an early start, and because it was able to take advantage of economies of scale, it projected a cost of only $80 million for its millennium project.
>
> All was going well until early 1997, when United Healthcare acquired the American Association of Retired Persons' Medicare supplemental insurance business. From an insurance industry point of view, this was a huge coup. From a Y2K point of view, it created a huge challenge. The year 2000 repairs on the newly acquired part of the business are costing substantially more per line than the original project did.

- Uncommon equipment or computer languages mean increased costs. The more widely used your systems are, the easier it is to find programmers with the expertise to fix them—as well as automated software tools to help the programmers. Thus, IBM mainframes, IBM-type personal computers, Apple computers, and DOS and UNIX-based systems should be fairly straightforward to repair or upgrade with year 2000-compliant software provided by vendors.

You're likely to have a bigger problem if your computer systems are highly unusual or were specifically built for your industry or company, or if you're working in more specialized languages. You may also have trouble if you're working with "orphan" hardware or software made by a company that has since gone out of business. Any of these factors can increase the difficulty, and raise the cost of a year 2000 repair.

Dealing with lost source code is expensive. In Chapter Two, I described the problem of missing source code (cases where the original human-written program is lost, and only the machine code, which runs on the actual computer but is incomprehensible to a human, remains). The Gartner Group estimates that 10 percent of the programming currently in use worldwide has missing source. If your company has had its own in-house software for five years or more, chances are some of your source code is missing.

Generally speaking, the two solutions to a missing source problem are either to have a vendor company convert the machine code back to source code—so it can then be examined for year 2000 glitches—or to rewrite the program from scratch and make sure that it is year 2000-compliant. The second option may seem more appealing, but if, this close to the millennium deadline, you're dealing with missing source, chances are you only have time for the first option. Either way, missing source adds to the cost of a year 2000 repair.

Can Costs Be Controlled?

Fixing the year 2000 problem is an expensive project that your company can't afford *not* to do. At this late date, you may not have much choice about how much you spend to do it. But there are some measures that may still offer a little cost relief.

Severe Triage

One obvious way to cut the cost of fixing a system is not to fix it at all. This is clearly not a decision you can make in every case. Hopefully, by this time you're past the triage phase of your project.

But, as we have seen, it's a virtual certainty that some of your organization's systems will not be repaired in time, no matter how much you spend. So it's a good idea to make cost cutting part of the equation when you consider what to fix and what to leave. Some problems (like the disappearing accounts described in the Introduction) will fix themselves in a few years, as the computer stops trying to make calculations that cross over the 99–00 threshold. Other systems, such as payroll, can readily be outsourced, and doing so might be less costly than fixing them. In still other cases, you may decide that a date of 1900 rather than 2000 on an internal document is something you can live with.

The Two-Digit Fix

At the programming level, there are two ways to correct a year 2000 problem. One is to rewrite the program so that the year is represented by a four-digit field instead of a two-digit field. This means profoundly changing the program, and although it is the clearest and most permanent solution to a year 2000 problem, it is also the most expensive—and the most time-consuming.

For both those reasons, more and more companies with less time and money to spend on Y2K are using another type of solution that is quick and dirty, as programmers say, but a lot faster and cheaper. That is to insert an IF . . . THEN statement into the program that allows it to keep using two-digit year fields and make an educated guess as to which century they refer to.

It works like this: Let's say your company has been in business for sixty years and is dealing with thirty-year mortgages. In no case will your software ever have to look more than sixty years into the past, or thirty years into the future. Thus, the earliest year that could exist on your system is 1939, and the latest is 2029.

In this situation, you could insert a simple equation into your programs to convert two-digit years to four-digit years:

If nn [two-digit year] is equal to or greater than 38, then nn equals 19nn. If nn is less than 38, then nn equals 20nn.

When software developers refer to "windowing," "procedural," "masking," or "interpretation" year 2000 changes, this is what they mean. The four-digit fix is usually called "field expansion." Because windowing[4] is both much cheaper and much quicker, the Gartner Group reports that 80 percent of the companies it's tracking are using it in at least some of their systems.

The two-digit solution does have obvious drawbacks, however. First of all, it can only be applied in some cases. A database that included the years houses were built, for example, could not guess in 2002 whether "02" meant 1902 or 2002. Second, it is not a permanent solution. In the mortgage example above, the fix stops working in 2009, as the company begins writing mortgages that reach into 2039.

Of course, 2008 is a decade away. Both hardware and software are developing so rapidly that there's a good chance the mortgage software will be either obsolete or easily upgraded by the time the 2039 date is needed. In any case, there's plenty of time to worry about it before then. On the other hand, it was thinking just like this that created the year 2000 problem in the first place.

A third possibility, called "date compression," is to make complete information about the day and year fit into six digits. There a few ways of doing this, but one obvious one is to start with the assumption that January 1, 1900, was day one; January 2 was day two; and so on. Including leap years, the century thus counted only amounts to 36,525 days, a total that falls well short of a six-digit number. So far, however, such methods run a distant third to field expansion and windowing.

Eliminating Dead Code

I discussed the problem of dead code (code that exists within your program but is never in use) in Chapter Two. Identifying and eliminating dead code is one way to reduce the cost of a year 2000 repair, not to mention the wasted time and effort required to reprogram code that doesn't need it.

Capers Jones suggests that companies assume that dead code, blank lines, and comment lines (which provide information to those reading the program but are not actually executed on the computer) make up about 30 percent of the total volume of code. If you're working with an outside vendor, he notes, those lines should not be figured into your repair costs since they won't need to be repaired.

Automation

As previously discussed, there is no silver bullet software that eliminates the year 2000 problem with no human labor. But this doesn't mean there are no programs that can help. To whatever degree you can use software to conduct your year 2000 fix, you probably save both time and money.

Chances are, you also wind up with greater accuracy. The actual work of year 2000 reprogramming is, among other things, incredibly boring. The longer a human programmer has to spend doing it, the greater the likelihood of his or her mind wandering. Accuracy is particularly crucial for the biggest part of a Y2K project: testing. Unfortunately, there are fewer software solutions for testing than for any other part of the project.

This shortage has actually inspired some intrepid companies to write their own testing software. That's what UK-based NatWest Bank (formerly National Westminster) did. According to NatWest's chief information technology officer, Achi Racov, hand testing would have been "a disaster, both in terms of time and of cost." On the other hand, creating the software from scratch was no picnic. "People told us that what we wanted to do was not possible, and they were close to being right," he says. He's not sure he would undertake such a project a second time.[5]

Sending Work Offshore

Cost savings is one big reason why many companies faced with a year 2000 project are sending some of their programming work to less-developed countries like India, the Philippines, and Ireland, as well as many of the countries of Eastern Europe, usually via a vendor with offices in the United States. A second benefit of this offshore outsourcing is that time zone differences allow these programmers to work on American computers during hours when offices here are closed. They can thus avoid overtaxing and slowing down the systems. (However, this requires giving outsiders network access, which some companies may be reluctant to do.)

Cost savings can be substantial. Analysts here assume costs of more than $8,000 a month in salary and benefits for a programmer working on Y2K, while vendors in India (which is currently dominating the offshore year 2000 market) report monthly costs as low as $1,000.

Of course, the potential quality control, communications, and cultural problems inherent in sending any work overseas exist in this case as well. If the work is traveling back and forth over the Internet or another telephone-based system, it might be a good idea to have a backup plan on hand, in case year 2000 glitches interrupt telecommunications. But given the shortage of qualified programmers here, at least there should be fewer complaints about depriving Americans of work.

Reporting Year 2000 Costs

Beyond the question of how much your company must spend to fix the year 2000 problem is the question of how it records those expenses. Few aspects of Y2K are simple and straightforward, and unfortunately, accounting is not among them.

In the summer of 1996, the Emerging Issues Task Force of the Financial Accounting and Standards Board (FASB) determined that money spent to fix the year 2000 problem should be listed as an expense during the year it was spent. The only problem with this is that what FASB decrees governs corporate financial statements and SEC filings. It does not have any bearing on how your company reports these expenses for tax purposes. Those questions are governed by the Internal Revenue Code, according to which the year 2000 fixes most often fall into the category of capital expenditures, which must be amortized over several years. This leaves you with the worst of all possible combinations: reporting Y2K expenses in the current year on financial statements to shareholders and banks, and amortizing them for tax purposes.

Bad enough, but things can get even worse when you consider section 482 of the Internal Revenue Code. It states that if one division of a group of related corporations (such as a conglomerate) performs technical services that benefit other divisions, those technical services can be treated by the IRS as taxable income for the benefiting divisions.

This bit of law is very bad news for large or decentralized organizations facing year 2000 repairs. Year 2000 project managers agree that the only way for any organization to avoid serious Y2K trouble is to manage its project from a single, central office. The reasoning here is twofold. First, this way one office has both full responsibility for the success of the project and full knowledge of how it is progressing throughout the organization. Second, this way the company takes advantage of whatever efficiencies can be gained by using the same software tools and strategies throughout the organization. (The fact that the federal government is *not* managing its year 2000 project in this manner is one reason expert observers are expecting it to fail!)

This presents an enormous problem, though: If you manage your Y2K project in the most effective way, you may have to pay extra taxes for having done so!

A little bit of hope is offered by two provisions of the tax law. The first allows deductions for repairs that neither materially add to the value of a property nor appreciably prolong its life. In August 1998, the IRS did announce that it would allow same-year deductions for year 2000 repairs, but not for improvements of any sort. However, distinguishing repairs from improvements might be harder than it sounds. "It's going to be a fine and fuzzy line between improving your software and converting it," tax attorney Hannah Carvey told the Associated Press. "When you actually get into it, there's very little you can buy that doesn't actually improve your system."[6]

The second question is whether year 2000 repairs can be qualified as research and development costs. As such, they may also be deductible, but meeting the requirements for a deductible research expense is a complex matter, best undertaken with highly qualified tax advice.

One of the more problematic elements of this tactic is that according to the Internal Revenue Code, research expenses must be incurred by the taxpayer, or *"upon the taxpayer's order and at his risk."* This means that if you use an outside vendor to work on your year 2000 problem, you cannot have a warranty that the repairs will work. If you do, the repairs are no longer at your risk, and you stand to lose your chance to deduct these costs as R&D expenses.

Think this all sounds unfair? Lawmakers may agree. Some executives, lawyers, and accountants struggling with questions of reporting Y2K expenses are hoping that Congress takes up this issue and writes new laws to clarify how year 2000 expenses are to be deducted—hopefully in the year they are incurred. Given the threat this problem poses to the very survival of a business, it seems like a reasonable hope.

As this book is being written, Rep. Karen Thurman (D-Fla.) has just introduced a bill that offers small businesses up to $20,000 in tax deductions for year 2000 expenses. This may be a step in a helpful direction, but it's only one step and still far from becoming an actual law.

In any case, whatever Congress decides, it's wise to involve tax planning experts as of the earliest stages of your Y2K project. They can help make sure contracts and other documents are properly worded to give your company its best chance of same-year deductions for year 2000 expenses.

Notes

1. Capers Jones, *The Year 2000 Software Problem: Quantifying the Costs and Assessing the Consequences* (Addison Wesley, 1997). (See Recommended Other Reading.)

2. Ed Yardeni, Ph.D., *Y2K Reporter*, March 1998. (See Recommended Other Reading.)
3. Minda Zetlin, "Countdown to Trouble," *Management Review*, American Management Association (May 1997).
4. Throughout this book, the term *windowing* is understood in the specific sense defined in the Glossary and bears no relation to any Microsoft Windows personal computer product or similar usage.
5. Zetlin.
6. Curt Anderson, "Firms May Deduct Cost of Y2K Bug," Associated Press (August 14, 1998).

CHAPTER 6

The Glitch That Launched a Thousand Lawsuits

"A few months back I read an article that said securities lawyers were salivating over the prospect of shareholder suits on year 2000 problems. Well, we get involved on securities suits, and we know a lot of securities lawyers, and I can assure you that they're not salivating. They are slobbering!"

—STEVEN L. HOCK, MANAGING PARTNER OF OPERATIONS, THELEN, MARRIN, JOHNSON & BRIDGES

If the numbers in the last chapter seem imposing, keep in mind that most of them don't take into account one of the most expensive aspects of the year 2000 problem: lawsuits. Like year 2000 malfunctions themselves, Y2K lawsuits are not a matter of speculation; they are already happening. And, like year 2000 malfunctions, they grow exponentially as we approach the turn of the century. Here are just a few instances of events that have already led to legal action.

> A factory line was shut down for lack of a component product. Come to find out, the product had been delivered on schedule, but because it had a two-digit expiration year starting with zero, it was automatically rejected by the factory's computer. The manufacturer sued the supplier, and the case was settled out of court.

> Because of an unremedied year 2000 problem, a department store chain's central processing mainframe glitched. As a result, the stores were unable to process credit card information for three months. Business suffered, stock prices plummeted, and the shareholders of the company sued its officers for negligence in their failure to deal with Y2K. This case, so far as I know, remains unresolved.

> A software vendor used the slogan "Software you'll never outgrow." Now it wishes it hadn't. You guessed it: The software that purchasers would supposedly never outgrow won't work in the year 2000. The resulting class action suit remains unresolved.

Estimating overall costs for year 2000-related lawsuits is an even vaguer science than estimating costs for year 2000 repairs. Capers Jones, for instance, guesstimates that the figure for Y2K legal fees might reach $2 billion in the United States, and that damages and punitive damages in this country might reach $100 billion. "Expressed another way," he writes, "a major bank, insurance company, or Fortune 500 company in general might expect to pay about $750,000 a year in year 2000 legal fees between 1997 and 2005."

Big as these numbers are, other estimates are even bigger. For instance, the Giga Information Group predicted in March 1997 that year 2000 litigation costs worldwide might be more than $1 trillion. As Jones notes: "On the whole, the results of litigation are unpredictable and therefore the overall impact of the year 2000 problem on litigation is really outside the scope of standard economic analysis. However, the number and seriousness of possible year 2000 lawsuits should cause every corporate executive and government official with software responsibilities to behave in a prudent fashion."[1]

It's easy to see why Y2K is a natural lawsuit producer: It's a huge problem, the stakes are very high, and everyone is looking for someone to blame. What may be less obvious is that many of these lawsuits might not directly involve computers or computer technology at all.

Consider this possibility. You're a caterer who supplies food to functions at an elegant hotel. You sign a contract to cater an important banquet for five hundred people. But on the day of the banquet, a Y2K glitch prevents your food distributor from delivering the ingredients you need, and you are unable to provide the meals you promised. The banquet's prestigious guests wind up sending out for two hundred pizzas. Not surprisingly, the hotel sues you and, since you are in breach of contract, wins easily. Your only recourse is to turn around and sue your distributor. However, the problem did not originate with your distributor's computer, but at a warehouse three states away that should have supplied your distributor with groceries. So your distributor must now sue the warehouse.

This scenario is a good example of how a company without an in-house year 2000 glitch (or even a computer!) can still feel the impact of Y2K. It also illustrates how such a company easily becomes a link in a seemingly endless chain of litigation. In fact, given the interdependent nature of today's business community, and the alacrity with which we seek legal remedies for our troubles, these domino-effect lawsuits seem a depressingly likely result of the year 2000.

But this is not the only result. A wide variety of legal actions are possible, from class-action lawsuits by customers who've been inconvenienced because of Y2K to—most frighteningly—lawsuits over deaths or injuries resulting from an unrepaired glitch. Could the year 2000 problem *really* cause injury or death? Hopefully, this will remain a theoretical question, but yes, it certainly could if, for example, a delicately controlled piece of computerized medical equipment malfunctions at a critical moment. Then, of course, comes the inevitable flood of lawsuits as software vendors, year 2000 consulting firms, and insurance companies sue and countersue each other in an effort to recover or defray part of the cost of dealing with the millennium glitch.

When Shareholders Sue

Publicly held companies whose earnings suffer because of the year 2000 problem, or that are forced to pay large sums to head it off, are certain to find themselves facing shareholder lawsuits. As I mentioned in Chapter Five, my computer has automatically flagged way too many accounts of lower-than-expected earnings or plummeting stock prices to doubt that many public companies are already feeling the effects of Y2K—and if I'm aware of these developments, these companies' stock owners must be doubly so.

In these cases, officers and directors of the company can be held personally liable for damages. Potential liability arises out of management's obligation to provide a management discussion and analysis of operations and trends (MD&A) as part of its 10K financial filings with the SEC. The MD&A should address all trends and conditions that can have a material effect on future financial results—a description that squarely fits the year 2000 problem.

Corporate officers can try to protect themselves by including some sort of boilerplate warning about Y2K disruptions and expenses. Many have done just that, though as I've noted earlier the information has been generally deemed insufficient by anyone familiar with this issue.

But the specter of shareholder lawsuits raises a difficult question—one that every organization should be prepared to answer without delay: Exactly who is an officer? Or, more precisely, who can be held accountable for year 2000 troubles? Whatever the answer, these are questions that should be addressed up front.

Chief information officers, who often have the most direct decision-making involvement with the year 2000 problem, have usually been considered outside the "directors and officers" group for the purposes of shareholder lawsuits. Besides, as a practical matter, as individuals they often lack the tremendous wealth that makes such an undertaking worthwhile for the plaintiffs. But all of this does not mean that CIOs and other technology workers involved in a year 2000 repair don't need legal advice and protection. In the likely event of a Y2K lawsuit, of any kind, they are almost certain to be subpoenaed to testify about whether their companies took the year 2000 seriously—and how seriously.

Unfortunately, if this happens, plaintiff's counsel may well put the situation in black-and-white terms: Either the technology worker screwed up by failing to appreciate the gravity of the year 2000 problem, or the officers screwed up when they failed to heed the technology worker's warnings. Which is it?

In these situations, many technology people will have an understandable desire to blame their bosses—especially because there's likely to be a grain of truth in this version. The fact is, most companies started dealing with this problem somewhat later than they should have, and few devoted the resources that were really needed early enough to prevent the risk of mishap.

According to Steven Goldberg, a litigation attorney at Cosgrove, Eisenberg & Kiley in Boston, the best solution is for employers to provide their CIOs, year 2000 project managers, and other key staff with both personal indemnification in case of year 2000 lawsuits and also their own lawyers, who, though paid by the company, act solely in the employee's interests.[2] This allows these key employees to concentrate on the task at hand, rather than worry about securing their own legal safety, and expert legal advice might help them avoid pointing the finger of blame at their companies.

Indeed, this is something savvy year 2000 project managers and CIOs are negotiating now, while the legal outlook is still—relatively—calm.

Unexpected Worries

Unfortunately, you don't need to have a year 2000-related business disruption to get into legal hot water over Y2K. For instance, one area you might not immediately think would be a problem is the copyrights on any software you may be using, especially if it turns out not to be year 2000-compliant.

Of course, one would logically expect that if the software doesn't work, you are more likely to sue the software vendor than the other way around. Although this is certainly true (more about this later), the reverse is also possible. Here's how.

You find that a piece of software you use regularly is not year 2000-compliant. Since your company has a well-organized Y2K project, with a staff of programmers in house, you hand the software to them for year 2000 remediation. Well and good—except that if your company has only licensed the software and doesn't own the actual copyright, you've just violated federal law. This is because the holder of a copyright owns the exclusive right to create derivative work; in past software-copyright cases, software upgrades and revisions have been defined as derivative works. This means that your repair of this software could be seen as copyright infringement. Not only that, rewriting the software may also void any guarantees or warranties you have on it.

Obviously, you need to be able to upgrade your organization's software to bring it into year 2000 compliance—or you might as well throw it away when 2000 arrives. The best solution, if you want to make these repairs yourself, is to secure the copyright holder's permission before you start. Even if you can't, your good-faith effort to get it might still serve as an argument in your favor if the issue ever goes to court.

A second problem involves software licensing, since licenses are often granted for a limited period of time. Thus, year 2000 project managers have sometimes reported "aging" a piece of software to see if it will function properly in the year 2000, only to find that it doesn't work at all—not because of the millennium glitch but because the current licensing period expires before then. This problem can usually be solved by getting a special extension from the software vendor. But it adds an extra step to the process.

Can We Talk?

Another issue some companies have raised concerns antitrust laws, which limit the amount of information companies can share with their competitors. In such industries as air travel and finance, where competitors' computer systems must work together in perfect synchronization, withholding information like this is a recipe for year 2000 disaster.

The good news is, the government thinks so too. Both John Koskinen, the Clinton administration's year 2000 czar, and Joel Klein, head of the Justice Department's antitrust division, have gone out of their way to reassure business leaders on this point. "If they're truly sharing information to fix this problem, that by itself is not a violation of antitrust laws," Koskinen told reporters recently.[3] However, according to one Justice Department official, if information sharing gets into such sensitive areas as how Y2K repairs might affect pricing or customer relationships, individual companies should proceed carefully, preferably with legal advice.

The Justice Department also issued the first of a planned series of industry-specific advisories on this matter, in response to a request from the Securities Industry Association. Financial firms, which must work together with lightning speed, have been generally ahead of the game in addressing the year 2000 problem and have for the most part worked cooperatively on the problem, since any firm that can't properly execute computerized trades threatens all of Wall Street. The SIA therefore proposed a plan to share both information about software tools that would help securities firms deal with the glitch as well as the results of the tests any member firm makes on these products—a move Klein has said is not anticompetitive and will not be met with legal action from Justice.[4]

The "Zippermouth" Strategy

But many companies are finding non-antitrust reasons to withhold information. At a recently held conference I heard one year 2000 consultant describe the situation this way: "In the early days, when we would ask our business partners for information on their year 2000 efforts, we would get very complete, helpful answers. When we've made these requests more recently, I think lawyers have gotten involved, and suddenly, it's zippermouth."

He is, I am certain, exactly right; lawyers have gotten involved. One of the things I find most dispiriting about the year 2000 problem is the apparent willingness of many companies to make problems for their suppliers and customers much worse than they need to be by refusing to share information these business partners have a legitimate need to know, to protect their own legal position.

Indeed, some legal advisors are taking the view that discussing the year 2000 problem at all—even acknowledging its existence—can put a company at a disadvantage. One lawyer quietly explained to me that if a client company is so far behind in its Y2K repairs that there is no hope whatsoever of averting massive disruptions, he might advise its executives to take this hear-no-evil stance, since their only hope of a legal defense is the claim that they didn't know anything about the year 2000 problem.

I have two words for this legal position: fat chance! Y2K has been on the cover of *BusinessWeek*, on the "Oprah Winfrey" show, "Nightline," and every other major television and radio news show, and in every major newspaper around the world. Not only that, a recent survey by the Information Technology Association of America showed that one out of every four Americans is worried about the millennium glitch. Perhaps a sherpa who never left the peaks of Nepal could plausibly claim not to have heard of the year 2000 problem. But for a business executive to claim ignorance is preposterous. That would require such willful determination not to receive the news of the day in any form that the action in itself would constitute negligence.

Besides being bad legal strategy, the zippermouth approach is morally questionable. Refusing to share needed information in a timely fashion could actually prevent business partners from dealing effectively with their own Y2K dilemmas, or making alternate arrangements elsewhere for needed goods and services. In short, I believe anyone who would choose shortsighted legal protection over helping to actually solve the problem has his or her priorities seriously out of order.

The most egregious example I've ever encountered concerns the pacemaker industry, as described in Congressional testimony by the Giga Group. Though hospital tests indicate that pacemaker wearers need not worry that their hearts will stop on New Year's Eve 1999, pacemakers deliver the information they collect about a wearer's irregular heartbeats to medical computers, and the information is used in monitoring the patient and making treatment recommendations. It's easy to see how inaccurate information could lead to serious consequences.

This idea began worrying the Veteran's Administration about a year ago, and it set out to interview the nation's top five pacemaker manufacturers to see whether they knew about the problem and what, if anything, they were doing about it. Two of the five companies reported that they were working on the problem and would have it solved by 1998. Two more promised to have it solved by the year 2000—worrisome, given that information technology projects almost never meet their deadlines. But the fifth company would not even acknowledge that there *was* such a thing as a year 2000 problem. When the VA pushed for more information, the manufacturer flatly refused to discuss the matter.

Do you think this company is legally protected if someone wearing one of its pacemakers suffers a problem? If a malfunction in your product could prove fatal to a customer, is zippermouth a reasonable strategy?

Some help is on the way, in the form of "good Samaritan" legislation recently passed by Congress and signed by President Clinton. The proposed law protects companies from liability for giving out inaccurate information about their year 2000 compliance, dates for achieving compliance, or other Y2K information, as long as the inaccuracy arises from an honest mistake rather than intentional deceit. Some business leaders have requested that the law be broadened to also protect companies from liability for *accurate* information. Whatever form the law eventually takes, critics say it is not strong enough to bring much change in corporate behavior.

Staying Out of Trouble

If stonewalling is a bad idea, what are your best legal defenses against the likelihood of a year 2000 lawsuit?

One obvious measure is to make sure your organization's own Y2K problem is solved in time, so that your company cannot be responsible for disrupting anyone else's business. After all, the only worse place to be than in the middle of the litigation chain is on the end where the glitch created the original problem.

Unfortunately, as noted in Chapter One, some 80 percent of the world's businesses have started their projects too late to repair all their systems in time. If yours is among them, the next best thing, from a liability point of view, is to be able to prove that you tried your best. This is why it's important to keep written documentation of every step in the process of your Y2K fix. (Indeed, since most companies have found solving the year 2000 problem to be more difficult than it first seemed, you should probably keep documentation even if you currently believe all your repairs will be completed by the deadline.)

These records should demonstrate direct involvement with and commitment to fixing the year 2000 problem at the highest management levels in your organization. As Steven Hock explained during a presentation at a conference:

> The reason it's essential is that if you end up in a courtroom, the first thing the jury is going to want to know is, what efforts did top management make to solve this problem? If the answer is, "We don't have the documentation to show that," or "Our executive management was focusing on something else," the jury is going to be mad and you're going to pay for it. You'll end up with executive management on the stand, and some lawyer standing there with a set of violins, saying, "Which one of these fiddles were you playing while Rome was burning?"

A year ago, very few companies had top management's commitment to dealing with the year 2000 problem, let alone any documentation to show it. More recently, things have changed, perhaps partly because of the media attention I mentioned earlier. What I hear these days leads me to think that most top executives at least say that the year 2000 is a major priority, though they don't always put their money and manpower where their mouths are. Their commitment level will almost certainly grow as the year 2000 nears, but it can already be characterized as too late.

In any case, whatever degree of commitment top executives have to the year 2000 project should be as favorably documented as possible. When creating this documentation, you should keep in mind who its eventual readers might be. If it's rife with technical jargon such as "legacy system" and "windowing," or even such management terms as "partnering" and "benchmarking," you may only wind up confusing the very jury you were seeking to convince.

Block That E-Mail!

Just as important as the documentation you keep is the documentation you should be careful to *avoid* keeping. Hock warns about what he calls "writers of rogue memos and e-mails," who can destroy your defense to a year 2000 lawsuit before you ever have a Y2K malfunction:

> Someone comes back to their work station after a horrendous sixteen-hour day, working on a major conversion project that's four weeks behind schedule. That person proceeds to pour out his or her heart in some memo or e-mail that resides on a hard disk somewhere. It starts with the name of the president of the company, and then it says: "This guy is out of it, he won't pay attention to our year 2000 problem. He will not do what's necessary to get this fixed. We're screwing up this project major league, it's going to cost our customers millions, and I'm the only one here who knows it!" Then that person feels better, goes home, and gets some sleep.

The problem is that what otherwise amounts to harmless venting can wind up costing you millions during a year 2000-related lawsuit. An early part of any such action is discovery, in which your opponent's lawyers have the right to examine all of your company's records and documents. Suddenly, e-mails and other messages that their writers believed totally private could be open to hostile view. Even e-mails that you've deleted from your computer's hard drive can sometimes be recovered.

What can you do to prevent these damning pieces of evidence from being written? For one thing, make sure anyone in a position to write such a document thoroughly understands the calamity it could cause. Another strategy is to make one of your company's lawyers available (preferably someone friendly) and encourage your staff to send their memos and complaints to him or her, rather than anyone else. That way, your employees can let off steam whenever they have to, but their gripes are protected by rules of attorney-client privilege and thus not be subject to discovery.

Seek and Ye May Find

Confidentiality is only one reason why it's a good idea to include legal counsel in your year 2000 process from the beginning. They may also be able to find some hidden sources of help in dealing with your Y2K problem: your existing contracts with both hardware and software vendors.

In many cases, Hock says, a legal analysis of software vendor contracts reveals language that obligates them to participate in your year 2000 repair, or help defray its cost. (This could apply if the vendor warrants that the product will work for a given period of time, or in maintenance agreements, for example.) The analysis should include any supporting documents, such as sales brochures, that helped lead to the agreement.

If there are such obligations, the time to look for them is early rather than late. In cases like this, the law requires you to give the vendor adequate notice in proper legal form. Simply writing a letter demanding the vendor's cooperation does not constitute such notice. It could even cost you whatever rights you have.

Your legal counsel should also review all future contracts with software and hardware vendors to specifically address the question of year 2000 warranties and liability. Because these are not easy negotiations, many companies have left this issue unresolved, figuring they can deal with it at a later date. But to do so is to take a big risk for one simple reason: The year 2000 problem is now highly visible and widely recognized. If you sign a contract that fails to address a widely known problem, you risk the presumption that your Y2K malfunctions are your responsibility.

Everybody's Doing It

The outlook for suing software vendors is made more complicated by the fact that much of the first rush of year 2000 lawsuits focuses on them. Makers of software and even computerized cash registers have been sued because their products fail to deal with the year 2000. In addition, until recently Intuit, maker of the banking software Quicken, faced two class-action lawsuits because versions 5 and 6 do not properly recognize year 2000 transaction dates and the company has not provided a free upgrade. (Recently, a judge dismissed one of the suits because plaintiffs have not suffered any damages from malfunctioning software—yet. I'm no legal expert, but this reasoning sounds strange to me; users either do or do not have the right to have their software work in 2000, and if it can be properly proved that it won't, why force them to undergo malfunctions before resolving the issue?)

The fact that so many lawsuits center on software developers has led them, in turn, to seek legislative protection. A group of concerned businesses, high-tech and otherwise, have banded together to form the Year 2000 Legal Coalition, with the declared goal of preventing frivolous Y2K lawsuits. The coalition has sponsored legislation specifically protecting software and computer companies from year 2000 lawsuits, if they make good faith efforts to deal with the glitch.

At this writing, coalition-backed legislation was recently defeated in California, and is under consideration in New York state. Meanwhile, the group has introduced similar legislation at the federal level. There have also been reports of legislation introduced by various states to bar year 2000 lawsuits against the state itself. I suspect that by the time this book is published, some of these initiatives will have become law.

In the end, this may not be a bad thing. With whole law practices being assembled whose sole purpose is year 2000 litigation, and Y2K courses being offered in law schools, there are good arguments for the notion that the legal feeding frenzy over the year 2000 needs to be curbed—particularly if fear of being sued prevents companies from sharing helpful information. On the other hand, if top managers finally are taking the year 2000 seriously, liability worries are certainly one reason why.

A last piece of legal advice: Keep the year 2000 in mind if your company is engaging in a merger or acquisition between now and 2000. You could find yourself saddled with someone else's year 2000 problem, and solving it might throw your own carefully orchestrated project off schedule. A careful examination of your new acquisition's Y2K vulnerabilities should be part of the merger's due-diligence process. Indeed, Hock says, you should approach year 2000 due diligence in the same manner as environmental due diligence, "but with even greater care because the potential liabilities are larger."

You probably need expert help in determining just how much of a year 2000 problem the merger entails. In the meantime, your M&A contracts should contain Y2K warranties, indemnifications, and possibly an escape clause in case the acquisition company's year 2000 problem proves unmanageable.

Underwriting Y2K

When it comes to the question of insurance for the year 2000 problem, there's good news and bad news. The good news is that the same lawyers who carefully review your contracts with information technology providers should also take a look at your existing insurance contracts. Though they were probably not written with the year 2000 in mind, it's just possible that these contracts provide some Y2K coverage.

The idea is that altering computer data to accommodate needed changes to the system might constitute property damage, which is covered under many policies. It may be especially helpful if the policy covers "valuable business records."

That all or part of a year 2000 fix may be covered as property damage is nothing more than a legal theory at this point. But given the expense involved in most year 2000 fixes, it's certain that sooner or later some enterprising lawyer will put this theory to the test.

That, such as it is, is the good news. The bad news is that whatever coverage you can scrounge through creative interpretation of current and past insurance contracts might wind up being the only year 2000 insurance you ever have. At this writing, the insurance industry is grappling with the question of Y2K. The Insurance Services Office recently drafted a boilerplate year 2000 exclusion for use by its fifteen hundred insurer members. Insurers have also asked all fifty states to allow them to specifically exclude Y2K liabilities from their coverage. So far, forty-six have agreed, and the last four are considering the request. Many insurance companies have already specified Y2K exclusions in their 1999 commercial contracts, but many others have not, for three reasons:

1. Insurance is a buyer's market, and they fear driving commercial customers away to competing insurers that do not specifically exclude year 2000 costs.
2. Since the calendar year 2000 is anything but an unexpected occurrence, many insurers have taken the position that—with or without a specific exclusion—most Y2K-related expenses aren't covered anyway.
3. Thus, they fear that using the exclusion weakens argument two by creating the presumption that coverage *was* included in the policy until the exclusion was added.

Are you covered? Are you not covered? In the absence of a specific exclusion, as a general once said of a battle, "the situation is confused." I believe it will take several lawsuits to settle matters before there is a clear answer to this question.

If You Have a Few Million to Spare . . .

Meanwhile, a couple of insurance companies have stepped bravely into the new world of specific year 2000 coverage. American International Group (AIG) offered Y2K insurance of a sort, for a while. The sort is called "blended" or "finite" insurance, and it worked like this: Depending on your company's perceived Y2K risk, AIG charged 60–80 percent of the coverage bought. This means that if you wanted $100 million in insurance, the policy's premium cost between $60 and $80 million. However, at the end of the coverage period (2002, say), AIG rebates 90 percent of the premium paid, minus whatever losses were actually incurred.

Even at that, AIG executive vice president Robert Omahne stressed that the company only wanted to sell a few of these policies, perhaps no more than fifty. And he meant it. At this writing, AIG has just announced that it will stop offering this insurance.

A few other insurance companies have developed special year 2000 products and services. One well-known example is 2000 Secure from insurance broker J&H Marsh & McLennan. As concern about the issue grows, so does interest in the product; the company says it received five applications in all of 1997 but is receiving one or two a week in 1998. Premiums range from 5 to 20 percent of the limit of liability, which means 2000 Secure may only be affordable to large companies. According to J&H Marsh & McLennan executives, the ultimate cost of coverage depends on an applicant's industry, revenue size, and the state of its year 2000 preparedness.

Y2K readiness is an important question for any company that wants year 2000 insurance—or, increasingly, any kind of insurance. More and more, with insurers as with lenders, expect stringent evaluation of your year 2000 status to be part of the deal. Many companies view this process as a giant pain in the neck, and understandably so. But it's also one more argument you can use to sell your top management on devoting the resources it takes to deal effectively with Y2K.

Notes

1. Capers Jones, *The Year 2000 Software Problem: Quantifying the Costs and Assessing the Consequences* (Addison Weley, 1997). (See Recommended Other Reading.)
2. Steven H. Goldberg, "Are You Indemnified Against Year/2000 Lawsuits?" *Year/2000 Journal* (May/June 1998). (See the online magazine at www.y2kjournal.com.)
3. Rajiv Chandrasekaran, "Trustbusters to Address Year 2000 Fix," *Washington Post* (June 2, 1998).
4. Ibid.

CHAPTER 7

Too Many Programs, Not Enough Programmers

"I was speaking at a year 2000 conference recently, and I asked audience members if any of them had managed to hire a substantial number of programmers lately. One man raised his hand and, with a big smile, said he'd just hired eighteen of them. Another member of the audience had such a look of shock on his face that I had to ask him how many programmers he had just lost. 'Eighteen,' he answered. It's a zero-sum game."

—PETER DE JAGER

The year 2000 is more of a business problem than a technology problem. So it makes sense that the single biggest obstacle to a successful Y2K conversion project is not hardware, or even software, but finding—and keeping—the right people to do the job. Y2K is, among other things, a human resource challenge of major proportions.

Even if there were no year 2000 problem, corporate America would still be facing a severe shortage of technology workers. In early 1997—before most corporate and governmental year 2000 projects had really gotten off the ground—the Information Technology Association of America showed there were about 190,000 unfilled technology positions in the United states. ITAA's response was to call for Congress to examine the problem and create a national skills training program for technology workers. Sen. John

Warner (R-Va.) has established a commission to look into the problem. Indeed, massive retraining of American workers is an excellent idea, and similar programs have worked very successfully in other countries. But it certainly won't happen in time to help with Y2K.

Meanwhile, the technology worker shortage is growing exponentially. By early 1998, the ITAA found there were 340,000 unfilled jobs—an increase of nearly 80 percent. Beyond a doubt, some of this dramatic growth in unfilled jobs is a direct result of Y2K. Worse, the study was too early to show the effects of the euro conversion projects now in process in Western Europe and around the world, which push demand for qualified programmers even higher (more on this later in this chapter).

News reports of American headhunters traveling the world in search of programmers abound, and in 1997, for the first time the 65,000 work visas available for skilled foreign workers were completely used up. In 1998, Congress responded by increasing available visas for such workers to 115,000. This is, de Jager points out, another zero-sum game: Foreign countries can't spare programmers any better than the United States can.

Ultimately, there simply won't be enough IT people to do all the work that needs to be done; the ITAA has predicted that this shortage will hamper the future growth of many American companies. Although one could argue that the ITAA has a biased view of how important technology workers are to the success of American companies, there's no disputing the fact that mastering technology is becoming more and more essential to business success.

ITAA also predicted that the programmer shortage here would force American businesses to ship large amounts of programming work to other countries. This is already coming true for millions of lines of code that need year 2000 remediation, and one Y2K vendor from India was already predicting last year that the millennium date conversion would bring more than a billion dollars worth of programming work to his country alone.

Y2K Is Worse Than Most

Bad as the overall programmer shortage is, it's much worse where year 2000 projects are concerned. Why should this be? Here are a few reasons.

Y2K Is No Fun

David Kelble, the Wawa chain's year 2000 project manager, summed up the problem perfectly. He was talking to me about a mutual acquaintance who's been working on Wawa's year 2000 project for more than a year. "I know I'm going to lose him one of these days," Kelble said. "He's too good to be spending his time reprogramming dates."

In Chapter Two, I explained in some detail why finding and fixing six-digit date fields cannot be done by computer. Unfortunately, it's precisely the sort of task one would wish a computer could do: a tediously simple job that has to be repeated over and over and over. I've heard it compared to resetting the date on a never-ending series of VCRs.

Now, imagine you're a skilled programmer. You may not be qualified for all of the 340,000 IT jobs open across the country, but chances are you have a fairly wide range of options. Is this job description something you'd be likely to select? Before you answer, keep this in mind: Most year 2000 projects are already way behind, and they all face an immovable deadline. So if you work on one, you'll probably have to put in a lot of evening and weekend hours.

And it gets worse. Anyone who knows technology people knows that nothing excites them more than the prospect of working with the latest technology, the newest programs and programming languages. Working on a year 2000 project, by its very nature, means working with yesterday's technology and outdated programming languages running on outdated computer systems. Ed Yourdon comically illustrated this point at the American Management Association's Year 2000 Executive Forum by holding up an imaginary software project in front of his longtime friend and IT colleague Norbert Kubilus. "You say: 'Java! Java! Java!'" Yourdon intoned. "And look! You can see Norb starting to quiver already. Now try saying: 'COBOL! COBOL! COBOL!' See? Nothing's happening."

Knowledge of Ancient Languages Is Needed

Even if they like the idea of working in older languages, most young programmers don't know them. The biggest problem lies with COBOL, the "common business-oriented language" written specifically for business applications and used on mainframe computers, that was very popular in the 1970s and 1980s. COBOL has proved useful and durable, and it now accounts for more than half the lines of code in use worldwide.

Obviously, not all year 2000 conversion jobs need to be done in COBOL. But this language makes up such a big piece of the pie that Y2K software developers and consultants routinely focus on it to the exclusion of all others. Unfortunately, COBOL is now considered obsolete by many IT professionals. It has its staunch defenders, who praise its easy-to-understand construction and point to widespread prevalence as proof of its long-term survival. I don't doubt that COBOL programs will be with us for a long, long time, but the fact remains that most universities stopped teaching the language years ago. The emphasis these days is on client/server (rather than mainframe) technology, networks, intranets, the Internet, and programming in languages like UNIX and Java.

What all this adds up to is a huge demand for COBOL programmers to work on the year 2000 problem, a limited supply available to do the job, and no prospect of new ones among the crop of graduating college seniors. (I should add that COBOL is only the most widely used of several languages that are no longer taught in colleges but are needed for the year 2000 fix. FORTRAN is one other example of the same phenomenon.)

Here Comes the Euro

The only thing that could possibly make the year 2000 programmer shortage worse would be another major software conversion project that a significant portion of the world's companies and organizations have to undertake, in which many of the same applications have to be reprogrammed but in a completely different way, so that there is little to be gained by doing both at once. If this hypothetical project had a similar deadline to the year 2000 conversion, the disaster would be pretty much complete.

Unfortunately, it isn't hypothetical. All of the above is true of the introduction of the euro, the new cross-border monetary unit that eleven countries of the European Union are scheduled to start using in 1999, with other countries to join them over the next few years. Putting the euro into use means retooling a tremendous amount of software for financial companies, governments, and pretty much any other organization doing business in Europe today.

It also means rewriting currency conversion software, even for transactions that don't include euros, because European Union rules require that any currency conversions among euro-using countries be made using the euro as a sort of monetary middleman. This means, for instance, that software that once converted francs directly into marks must now convert the francs into euros (rounding to the nearest denomination) and then the euros into marks.

The first deadline for the transition to the euro comes in 1999, with other deadlines in 2002. This means that the lion's share of euro conversion reprogramming needs to be done at a time when many IT departments and people are already busy with the year 2000 problem. Because of this, many technology experts have loudly questioned the wisdom of introducing the euro now. One thing's for certain: The shortage of qualified programmers is going to get a lot worse before it gets better, assuming it ever does.

Expect to Pay Top Dollar

There's a new T-shirt rumored to be in circulation: "COBOL programmers are back, and we're mad!" The joke is based on fact. Computing conferences abound with stories of retired COBOL programmers lured off the golf course with promises of six-figure salaries.

Younger programmers can almost name their own wages as well. "I don't know if you're having trouble hiring people, but I am," John Bruns, manager, administrative systems at McCormick & Company, told an audience of IT managers at a conference a year ago. He went on to describe his encounter with a twenty-six-year-old COBOL programmer who refused to work for less than $120,000 a year. Outraged, Bruns sent her on her way. "I just didn't think a twenty-six-year-old, with only six years' work experience, had the stature to command that kind of salary," he says. "But somebody will pay it."

The Gartner Group has estimated that year 2000 repair costs will go up 20–25 percent a year between 1997 and 2000, and rising compensation for programmers is the reason for the expected increase. It's hard to predict how high these bidding wars might go.

But worse than driving up the cost of your year 2000 repair, the programmer crunch can derail it altogether if key personnel are tempted away to other jobs. In fact, according to Peter de Jager, smart companies are working on the assumption that this will happen. He believes it's prudent to plan for a 10 percent turnover of year 2000 staff—every month.

How Project Managers Can Cope

If you're in charge of a year 2000 conversion effort, these statistics can be pretty scary. I'm not going to kid you by saying that hiring and retaining qualified programmers for the project is likely to be easy, when it obviously isn't. But there are some things you can do to make it easier.

You'll be best equipped to deal with this problem if you go into your year 2000 project with the understanding that hiring qualified people is difficult, and that your organization will see some defections.

From this perspective, it's clear that your HR executives should be heavily involved in your year 2000 project as early in the process as possible. Your best defense against the talent shortage is to create a carefully planned and delineated human resource strategy that specifically addresses this challenge. This strategy should find ways to motivate and retain programmers and other information technology staff, and the project managers and other executives involved in overseeing, coordinating, controlling, and tracking the project. Here are some options to consider.

Cash Rewards for Year 2000 Performance

Wisely, many companies are hesitant to give lavish raises to IT professionals involved in Y2K projects because doing so creates an awkward situation later, after the project is done. On the other hand, as Bruns noted, if *you* don't come across with the big bucks, chances are someone else will.

What can you do? One solution is to offer money in the form of one-time bonuses or incentives. The information services area as a whole has been slow to adopt the sort of performance incentives that other disciplines (most obviously sales) have long used to boost their personnel performance. But this situation deserves to change, and the year 2000 project is an excellent place to start.

In "Compensation and Year 2000," an article in the *Year/2000 Journal,* Dave Bettinger, director of business solutions for CST2000 in Portland, Maine, proposes an individualized set of incentives for everyone working on the year 2000 fix. In addition to their regular salary and benefits, employees should be offered rewards at specific milestones during the life of the project, as well as a significant bonus if they stay on until the work is completed.

In Bettinger's model, a prototypical programmer earning $40,000 a year (but able to substantially increase that salary by leaving for another company) would be offered a $10,000 bonus for signing on to the Y2K project. For every project milestone that she delivers a month or more ahead of schedule, she receives another $10,000. She gets $5,000 if the milestone is on time, and no bonus if it is late. Once the entire project is completed, she receives $20,000 for finishing on time, $15,000 if less than a month late, $10,000 if less than two months late, and no bonus if it is later than that.

This may sound like a lot of bother, not to mention a lot of money, but it's certainly both more expensive and more bothersome to hire someone new and bring that person up to speed if members of your Y2K staff leave for other jobs. This is why many of the companies that are taking a strong approach to Y2K have included some form of reward system in their plans. Some advocate offering a 100 percent bonus—in other words, an entire year's salary—to IT staff who stay on throughout an entire year 2000 project.

Rewards for Non-Year 2000 Staffers

Putting a lucrative reward system in place for your Y2K staff can be a double-edged sword. You might gain greater loyalty and enthusiasm from those who are working on the project but alienate their colleagues who are at work on ongoing software maintenance—which is also something your organization can't get along without.

This is why Bettinger recommends using Y2K as an impetus to bring rewards-based compensation to your whole IT operation.

Noncash Rewards

It's trite, but true: Noncash rewards can be very powerful motivators, especially if used in conjunction with cash ones. There's a Volkswagen commercial airing these days in which a programmer comments that "when you write code for sixteen hours a day" you have to cut loose.

Kelble took this idea to heart and invited his year 2000 staff to a stock-car rally. Simpler rewards can include such things as plaques, gift certificates, or special mugs for completing portions of a year 2000 project. (I used to think the idea that such things motivate was hogwash, but recently, to mark the one-year anniversary of a Web magazine I write for, the publisher sent me a mug, emblazoned with its very lovely logo, filled with Hershey's kisses, and tied up with a big purple bow. I was unbelievably pleased.)

More meaningful rewards might include increased responsibility or the opportunity to work more flexible hours. Whatever motivators you choose to use, this is the time to pay some close attention to team building among your technology workers, especially if you have not done so in the past.

Training Opportunities

Programmers—especially those working in outdated languages like COBOL—may well be wondering what will become of them after the year 2000. This is a very good question.

The computer industry is changing so rapidly that it's a challenge for anyone, whatever his or her responsibilities, to stay up-to-date. For someone reworking an antiquated system as part of a more-than-full-time year 2000 project, the chances of keeping up with changing technology are nil.

Assuming these are people with a career commitment to computing, and not retirees adding to their nest egg or (as some rumors have it) Ivy League graduates who've found a quick way to pay off their student loans, your year 2000 staff is likely to be very behind the times by the time this project is over. With this in mind, you can see how the promise of extensive training could be a powerful incentive for technology professionals at work on the year 2000 project, especially because such ongoing training is often unaffordable to individuals. It would also show them that your company is committed to them for more than just the next couple of years.

Year 2000 project managers have less to worry about in this regard. Assuming their responsibilities are more managerial than technical, they are less likely to fall behind the times, and the expertise they gain by working on this complex and difficult project will stand them in good stead throughout their careers. But extra management training, as well as year 2000-related training, is a good idea for managers too. If that's you, and your top management recognizes that your job is truly essential, getting the training you want and need for yourself shouldn't be a problem.

Overstaffing

One of the few things less appealing than the thought of hiring a COBOL programmer at $120,000 a year is the thought of hiring two of them. But if your organization is dependent on its computing power, you should probably consider doing just that. Even if de Jager's prediction of 10 percent a month attrition proves to be too pessimistic, your department will almost certainly suffer from some loss. Having more staff than you strictly need can help ensure that all the work is done in time. Since year 2000 projects routinely turn out to be many times more complex than they appear at first, there's an excellent chance that there's plenty of work to go around. An interesting variant, especially for those on the management side of the project, is to keep some non-year 2000 staff members peripherally involved so that they can step in to fill a sudden vacancy.

Using Nonprogrammers as Programmers

As the shortage of qualified programmers becomes more and more dire, de Jager has come up with an interesting proposition: using people who aren't trained as programmers to work on the year 2000 project. He advocates identifying "power users"—clerical or other employees who are comfortable with their computers and tend to do such things as write their own macros. These people, he believes, can be quickly taught to do the more brainless year 2000 tasks and, with proper supervision, can help keep a project on schedule.

Franklin D. Roosevelt once said, in reference to the Great Depression, "Above all, try something." The sentiment applies here as well. Whatever strategy you adopt to deal with the shortage of information technology professionals, your worst choice is to do nothing in the hope that business continues as usual.

As this book goes to press, concern about Y2K is building fast in the media and throughout corporate America. Companies that are seriously behind in dealing with this problem (at least 80 percent, according to most estimates) are waking up in a panic to the realization that the year 2000 can mean real trouble for their organizations, and that they are running out of time to do something about it.

Bill Ulrich, coauthor of *The Year 2000 Software Crisis* (with Ian Hayes), has predicted that companies that failed to take the year 2000 seriously when they had the chance will be starting to panic outright at about the time this book comes out. That panic is likely to create a feeding frenzy, with increasingly desperate companies willing to pay almost anything for help with what they finally understand is a business survival issue. If you are not prepared, you will almost certainly lose key IT personnel during your own year 2000 project—when you can least afford it.

Is It Too Late to Learn COBOL?

There's no question that the shortage of COBOL programmers is a real opportunity for anyone who needs to make a lot of money quickly. But, with less than a year left until the year 2000, is it still worth taking the trouble to learn?

The answer is yes. Software experts are now predicting that year 2000 remediation will go on into the new millennium; some even believe these efforts will continue until 2005. Further, the euro conversion I mentioned earlier is also creating a demand for COBOL programming, and these projects are likely to continue for several years longer than most year 2000 projects. In any case, as COBOL proponents are quick to point out, there's a lot of new code being written in COBOL as well.

I believe the shortage of programmers in general, and COBOL programmers in particular, is a real boon for anyone who's comfortable working with computers and is between jobs or careers, or quickly needs to get on his or her financial feet. If this description fits you, then programming is certainly something you should consider.

Besides the chance to make a lot of money quickly, programming can provide a great deal of flexibility. A friend of mine is a musician who spends much of his time traveling from gig to gig. He's also a part-time programmer, and thanks to the Internet he can easily supplement his income by working on code between performances, no matter where he is.

It can also be a great entry to a technology career, especially if you're able to negotiate future training in more modern programming languages as part of your compensation package. Either way, there clearly are a lot of options.

Getting Outside Help

"Everyone who can print up a business card that says Year 2000 Consulting has done so. Some of them know what they're doing. Some of them don't."

—Ian Hayes, president of Clarity Consulting and coauthor (with William Ulrich) of *The Year 2000 Software Crisis*

With the year 2000 deadline drawing nearer, and the prospects of hiring extra IT staff looking grim, some businesses faced with Y2K are doing the logical thing: turning to outside consultants for help with their Y2K projects.

The consultants are out there. Hundreds of new Y2K consulting firms have started up since the problem first came to prominence in late 1994. Many of these are software development firms or consultants who've now made the year 2000 their special focus. The management consulting arms of the Big Six accounting firms are giving the year 2000 serious attention.

Most companies of any size at all are working with at least one vendor, and often three or more. It's easy to see why. An outside vendor can bring a variety of advantages to the project:

- *Flexible staffing*. For reasons just discussed, it may be difficult to hire all the programmers you need to solve the year 2000 problem. But if you do manage, you'll have another problem after the repair is completed and you no longer need quite so many of them. Though some degree of staffing up to deal with Y2K may still be necessary, working with a vendor can keep the numbers under control.

- *Availability of IT staff for other projects.* Conversely, whether you add staff or not, your in-house IT professionals will find their work schedules dominated by Y2K, for the year or more that the project lasts. Given the speed of technological advances today, two years is way too long to be out of the loop. You may get your year 2000 repair completed, but in the meantime your company will become technologically out-of-date.

- *More efficient tools.* IT people talk about finding "best of breed" tools (that is, software) to attack the year 2000 problem. Although there is no silver bullet, there are programs that can help, at least to some degree, at every stage of work. A vendor who has already been through the year 2000 repair process at other companies has probably experimented with a number of these tools and knows which ones work best.

- *Methodology.* An outside consultant likely to be familiar with different tools should also have worked out a method of attack for the year 2000. Remember that one of the hard parts of this job is figuring out which of several interconnected systems should be fixed first. A vendor who can answer questions like these is a valuable asset indeed.

- *Cost.* Though experts don't all agree on this point, some companies report that working with a vendor can provide savings over going it alone.

- *Sending work offshore.* Vendors can save you money in many ways, but one of the biggest is by arranging to have some of your Y2K work done in places like India,

Eastern Europe, Ireland, or the Philippines, where salaries are lower and there are more programmers available for the job. This practice is so common that most American year 2000 vendors work with offshore software conversion "factories" in these or other developing countries, and there are many offshore vendors with offices here as well. (Some pros and cons of offshore outsourcing are discussed in Chapter Five.) Needless to say, sending your work to a developing country is something you need a vendor's help to do.

Buying in a Seller's Market

Even though hiring a vendor to help with your company's year 2000 problem is clearly a good idea, finding one who is both willing and able to do the job is getting more difficult by the day. In 1996, the Big Six accounting firms were actively soliciting year 2000 business. By 1997, they were still accepting clients—selectively. As this book goes to press in the fall of 1998, the rumor is out that they are taking no new year 2000 clients, and even less well-known companies are turning away a lot of the work offered them.

Nevertheless, vendors have not all been getting booked up as quickly as expected. From the time the year 2000 problem first came to prominence, industry experts, including the Gartner Group, have been predicting that all vendors available to do year 2000 work will be completely booked up. Gartner's earliest predictions were that this would happen in 1997, but as I write this, it's the summer of 1998, and a recent ITAA survey shows that 75 percent of year 2000 vendors don't plan to start turning down business any time soon.

Does this mean you should stop worrying about vendor availability? Definitely not. I believe the unexpected capacity reflects both the growing crop of vendors that Ian Hayes colorfully describes above, and the fact that many organizations are waiting much too long to start on their year 2000 reprogramming. As this book appears, however, those who are dragging their heels must face the fact that they have run out of time. So if there is still vendor capacity available as you are reading this, chances are it won't be there for long. If you haven't yet hired all the outside help you need, I'd recommend setting down the book and picking up the phone right now.

The usual first step in selecting a contractor for a major project is to issue a request for a proposal. But unless RFPs are legally mandated for your company, you should consider skipping this step. For one thing, you don't have time. With a year to go until New Year's Eve 1999, your company may have just enough time to get its most essential systems fixed. This will certainly not be true, however, by the time you draft an RFP, send it out, evaluate the responses, and finally make your selection.

Even if you do have time to go through this whole process, chances are your prospective consultants don't. They're in an industry where demand is greater than supply. Presumably, they're hard at work, trying their best to accomplish a deeply complex project with a very short deadline for the clients they already have. If they're willing to respond to a detailed RFP, you might ask yourself why they have so much time on their hands.

Another common method for choosing a software development firm is to send the same sample project to several candidates. This may be a good way of making a comparison, but once again, it takes time you can't afford. Instead, Ian Hayes and Bill Ulrich suggest something more useful: sending a different part of the project to each prospective vendor, with clear specifications (so that each one's work is compatible with your post-Y2K systems). This allows you to make some progress on your year 2000 project while evaluating prospective vendors.

What to Look For

Assuming you still have some options when you seek out a year 2000 consultant, what qualities should you look for?

History With Your Company

Since the year 2000 is a business survival issue, you should have absolute trust in the people you hire to help you work on it. This is one reason why Prudential made a prior relationship one of its criteria for selecting Y2K vendors. Another good reason for doing this is the prospect that your two companies will continue to work together on other projects in the future.

"Some consultants have said, 'I'm going to make a lot of money over a couple of years, then I'm going to take off,'" Hayes reports. "Great! They'll be leaving just when these things are getting implemented."

The year 2000 problem is not going to end once the year 2000 arrives. Companies that rushed to get their most vital systems fixed will still have less crucial repairs waiting to be made. At least some of the newly repaired systems will turn out to have bugs or other problems that the repair itself creates. These are all good reasons why you need your vendor relationship to continue past December 31, 1999.

Reputation

If you can't, or don't want to, use a vendor you've worked with before, the next best thing is to find a company with solid standing in the industry. Managers working on Y2K are usually quite willing, and even eager, to share information, so gathering this information about prospective vendor firms should not be difficult.

It is also a plus if the firm in question has received Information Technology Association of America certification for its year 2000 methodology. Firms that gain certification first have their methods carefully audited by ITAA professionals.

Besides the company's reputation, that of the individual manager or managers who is responsible for your year 2000 project is of great importance. After all, even the best companies have some less-than-wonderful managers working for them. Don't forget to check this out too, as part of your evaluation process.

Good Subcontractor Relationships

Year 2000 projects are almost always more complicated than they appear at first. Yet the deadline for getting them done can't be moved. Given that combination, it's possible that well-meaning vendors might find themselves with more work than they can handle. You should know up front whether your consultant has good relationships with subcontractors in place, in case extra help is needed to complete your project on time.

Methodology

According to Hayes, the vendor you choose should have a well-thought-out, written methodology for managing a year 2000 project. "If they won't show it to you and let you look through it, then they don't have a methodology," he said at a recent conference.

Likewise, he notes, you should ask vendors which year 2000 software tools they work with. If they have some experience in the field, they should have some definite opinions about which software works most efficiently. Be wary of vendors who answer that they are happy to work with "whatever you've got."

You're Still Responsible

There are a range of formulas for working with year 2000 consultants. At one end of the scale, they might simply provide extra programming staff to work in your IT department, or training and information to get your project off the ground. Or, you may ask a contractor to completely take over one or more of your Y2K subprojects, or the entire project for your whole organization.

Even if you choose this last option, however, the ultimate responsibility rests with your company, and you still need people at your end to track and manage both the vendor relationship and the repairs themselves. This is why no matter how much outsourcing you do, if you want a year 2000 project to succeed, your company still needs its own project management person or team overseeing the effort.

As discussed in Chapter Five, there may be tax reasons why you wouldn't want to make a year 2000 vendor legally responsible for the success of your Y2K effort. If you do want to, it's hard to imagine a reputable year 2000 vendor agreeing to such an arrangement at this stage of the game.

But even if you do have a contract that makes your Y2K vendor responsible for mishaps, the ultimate responsibility for your firm's year 2000 problem is still yours. After all, having good grounds for a lawsuit is small consolation if your business is forced to close its doors because an essential system fails.

CHAPTER 8

Sharing the Pain

Business Partners and the Year 2000

"There are one million different parts in a [Boeing] 747. I learned that from a guy who makes them. I said, 'You don't make all those parts do you?' He said, 'Oh no!'

"There are thousands of manufacturers out there who make one product, and pass it up a chain, to another supplier, who then passes it to another supplier, who passes it to the manufacturing company that turns it into a car or an airplane or whatever.

"That's called the supply chain. Supply chains have ripple effects. You need to talk to your suppliers about their suppliers, about their suppliers."

—William Ulrich

Getting your company's year 2000 problem under control is difficult at best. Unfortunately, that's only half the job of preparing for the year 2000. The other half is dealing with the possibility of disruptions at the essential suppliers that keep your company in business.

As I write this chapter, in the summer of 1998, General Motors factories around the country have failed to produce more than two hundred thousand cars because of a six-week-old strike at two parts plants. This is a simple illustration of how interruptions in the supply chain can derail an otherwise well-functioning business.

Few aspects of the year 2000 problem have caused as much discomfort, legal wrangling, consternation—or paperwork—as this issue of determining preparedness among essential suppliers. This is also an area where it's absolutely necessary that a company's business managers, and not just technology people, get involved.

To begin getting a handle on this difficult issue, consider these questions.

Who Are Our Essential Suppliers?

This simple-sounding, but very serious, question is the starting point in your year 2000 supplier assessment. Because you are dealing with very sensitive and legally delicate issues (more about this in a moment), communications with suppliers on this subject should take into account not only how essential they are to your company's ability to function but also how important your businesses is to them.

How Much Trouble Are They In?

It can be difficult enough to evaluate your own company's year 2000 vulnerabilities, let alone someone else's. Yet this is what you must do, if you want to avoid risking supply chain problems.

If you're working with an independent year 2000 consultant, that organization can help. In fact, many of them do offer assessments of supplier firms, and there are good arguments for using this service. For one thing, since they're constantly examining Y2K efforts at a wide range of companies, they may be better able than you to judge whether a supplier is dangerously behind or not. Perhaps more important, as a third party they can take on the unpleasant tasks of delving into a supplier's activities and letting them know if they fall short of the mark.

Whether you use an outside consultant or not, keep in mind that there are three different ways a Y2K problem at a supplier organization can cause trouble for you. The first, and most obvious, is if the problem prevents them from delivering essential supplies or services when you need them. The second is if an unresolved problem of theirs causes a malfunction at your end because of electronic data transfers, or other problems, such as faulty expiration dates. The third is if year 2000-related disruptions or costs cause them to go out of business altogether.

Do They Know We Mean Business?

In 1996 and 1997, mention of the year 2000 as a serious business problem was as likely as not to be met with a chuckle and a roll of the eyes. In mid-1998, no one's laughing anymore. But neither are most businesses ready to accept this as a top-priority issue. Maybe they will be by the time this book appears. In any case, it's imperative that your suppliers understand that you take the possibility of year 2000-related disruptions very seriously and expect them to as well, if they want to keep your business. This is another case where an outside consultant can help you keep your relationship intact by taking on the "bad cop" role.

How Much Are We Willing to Help?

What if your worst fears are confirmed, and you find that one of your essential suppliers is threatened with a serious year 2000 problem? What should you do?

The millennium glitch can provide a real testing ground for the idea of business partnering. If the company in trouble is truly a partner, and is truly, as Steven Hock put it at a recent conference, "part of the circle of companies that makes us possible," you may want to extend a helping hand. An obvious first step is to share the information from your assessment, and give your reasons for thinking this company has a problem. This in itself might be enough to open some eyes. You could also share information on tools and methodologies, or even offer the services of your own Y2K consultant to help them get their project off the ground.

Ultimately, you may also find yourself tackling the difficult question of whether to extend financial aid. Year 2000 repairs can be brutally costly, and your supplier may not have the cash needed to pay for them. Unfortunately, banks are now evaluating Y2K readiness as part of their loan review process, creating something of a catch-22: A company that can't afford to fix its year 2000 problem may also be prevented from borrowing the funds to do so.

Make sure to subject the question to careful legal review before making any loans, however. In certain scenarios, a loan could make your company partly liable for the supplier firm's year 2000 mishaps.

What Are Our Alternatives?

What other suppliers can you use, if an essential supplier cannot deliver as promised? Now might be the time to put these backup relationships in place, in the likely event you find one or more supplier is at least potentially vulnerable to Y2K. Needless to say, these backup suppliers should also be assessed for year 2000 readiness. You might even ask for a guarantee that they'll be able to deliver in spite of Y2K—although such guarantees are increasingly difficult to get.

Should We Increase Inventory?

Does your company work on just-in-time inventory? If so, you are very vulnerable if one of your suppliers is prevented from delivering product on time (or at all) because of a year 2000 glitch. "If it doesn't arrive just-in-time, you're just out of luck," as one Y2K expert puts it.

As year 2000 approaches, it is wise to review some of your inventory arrangements. If these suppliers' year 2000 efforts do not pass a stringent examination, you should consider expanding your inventory temporarily, in case of a slowdown. Here, too, arranging for backup suppliers might be a good idea.

Remember that most just-in-time inventory processes work at least in part because computerization of ordering and delivery makes getting products from the supplier to your company a very efficient process. As the computers in question encounter the year 2000, that may suddenly no longer be true.

Will We Have Expiration-Date Problems?

It's easy to shrug off expiration dates as a simple year 2000 matter, partly because they're easy to understand, partly because sometimes they are funny—as when a prestigious magazine sent out subscription confirmations "good until 1901."

However, the most expensive and highly visible year 2000 malfunctions thus far have had to do with expiration dates. The best known of these was caused by issuance of Visa and MasterCards with expiration dates of "00" while many retailers' card readers were not ready to accept them. In another well-known case, the British department store Marks & Spencer repeatedly rejected a perfectly good shipment of corned beef hash because it carried an expiration date of 00; the store's computer concluded the product was more than ninety years old. Similarly, Kraft Foods accidentally destroyed millions of dollars worth of food because of two-digit expiration dates. If something like this happens to your company, it won't seem so funny.

Who Else Are We Dependent On?

For the purposes of Y2K, it's important to expand your concept of an essential supplier to include companies and organizations that you may not normally think of as suppliers but that still have the potential to cause serious business setbacks for you if they stop operating normally. Ask yourself what would happen if any of the following experienced a severe year 2000 disruption:

- The building where your company is located
- Your local utility
- Your local telephone company
- Your long-distance telephone company
- Your local transportation companies (buses, taxis, subways, etc.)
- The airline that serves your city
- Your delivery service (remember the effect of the UPS strike?)

In some cases, it may be quite appropriate for you to subject these "suppliers" to a year 2000 assessment—for example, in the case of your landlord or the management company for your building. In others, it may be harder to get answers. But in every case, you should consider what to do, and what alternatives you have, if there is a disruption of service.

How Will We Respond?

What will we say when our customers start asking all of the above about us? Count on it: They will. In fact, dealing with questions and assessments from customers is even more problematic than asking these questions yourself. The issues involved are complex and sometimes contradictory, and, as we will see in a moment, there may be no good answers.

Getting It in Writing

Like all aspects of the year 2000 problem, the legal ramifications surrounding these supplier-customer questions are something of a nightmare. Here are just a few aspects of the legal thicket.

- Your legal counsel may recommend that you ask suppliers to include in their contracts with you a guarantee that deliveries will not be interrupted because of a year 2000 malfunction. By the same token, you will probably be warned that under no circumstances should your company sign a contract that contains such a clause. Chances are, your suppliers and customers have gotten the exact same advice from *their* lawyers. This leads to interesting negotiations.

- Similar dilemmas arise when it comes to getting information on suppliers' year 2000 status. As a customer, you want to know everything, down to the last detail of your supplier's Y2K project. As a supplier, you may not want to tell your customers too much about what you're doing. There actually are lawyers advising their corporate clients to demand maximum information from the companies they do business with, while giving none themselves. This may be sound legal advice, but it's questionable as business practice.

- In particular, many lawyers warn never to guarantee that your company or product will be year 2000-compliant by a specific deadline. The odds of encountering unexpected trouble with your Y2K project, or other unplanned interruptions, are simply too great. If that happens, your guarantee may constitute a contract, and you could be sued for breaching it.

- On the other hand, some lawyers have argued that if you admit you are currently not year 2000-compliant—and can't say when you will be—this constitutes an "anticipatory" breach of your contract. In other words, you are announcing your intention not to live up to your obligations. In that case, business partners can go ahead and sue right now, without even bothering to wait and see if a year 2000 disruption actually occurs.

- Considering all this, it's not hard to understand why some companies are following the "zippermouth" strategy described in Chapter Six, refusing to discuss the year 2000 problem or even acknowledge its existence. But that's no solution either; pretending you don't know about Y2K doesn't seem very realistic, and withholding information could also get you into hot water.

- In Chapter Six, I described the new "good Samaritan" legislation that offers some measure of protection to companies sharing information on their year 2000 readiness. (President Clinton first proposed this law in a speech to the National Academy of Sciences on the very day I began drafting this chapter.) Whether the law offers enough protection to actually change corporate disclosure policies remains an open question.

- You probably have little legal recourse if you're faced with zipper-mouthed suppliers. You cannot compel them to reveal any information about Y2K's potential effects on their ability to deliver on time. Worse, if you have an existing contract with them and you take your business elsewhere because of their refusal to answer year 2000-related questions, you are in breach of contract.

Fighting Forms With Forms

By now, you're probably familiar with the letters many companies are sending out to try to elicit year 2000 information—many of them form letters, obviously being sent to dozens if not hundreds of suppliers. Indeed, it's highly possible your company is sending them out too. Many experienced Y2K managers report that what was once a trickle of these requests has now become such a flood that dealing with them is seriously limiting the efficiency of the project team, especially since many of these are questionnaires that could take anywhere from fifteen minutes to more than an hour to fill out.

Before worrying about how to deal with these things efficiently, back up for a moment and consider the question of just who is dealing with them. The people sending the letters naturally enough tend to send correspondence to whoever they already know at your company. That could be literally anyone on your staff.

As we have seen, the legal ramifications of giving out certain kinds of year 2000 information—especially in writing—can be serious indeed. So whatever you do, your first step should be to make sure these form letters and surveys are all conveyed directly to a responsible member or members of your Y2K team, and that they are the only ones who reply to them.

What should the replies look like? For many companies, one solution to the flood of information requests is to draft a form letter that serves as a reply to most queries. In some cases, it might make sense to offer several forms for different branches of your business, or different business functions. Since you may choose not to provide all the information a questionnaire asks for, this can also be a graceful way of sidestepping questions you're not willing to answer. Depending how much or how little information you include in your form, however, it may provoke real frustration on the other end.

Canadian Tire, in Toronto, has found an interesting alternative. In addition to sending out a form, the company offers more detailed year 2000 information on a password-protected Website. What does a business partner have to do to get a password? Share its own information with Canadian Tire.

Of course, a form letter isn't appropriate in all situations. A customer who accounts for, say, 50 percent of your business might be miffed, and rightly so, if a request for year 2000 information is answered only with a form letter. In cases like these, only a personal response will do. As a compromise measure, you could also note that the form letter is only intended to provide basic information; then invite recipients to call if they need more detailed answers.

The Tie-Lines That Bind

Questions of supplier compliance become much more complicated if you and they are in any sort of data transfer relationship—that is, if one or more computers at their site is connected by any sort of network to any of your computers, for ease of transferring any information, such as order details, back and forth.

In this case, you must not only know that they will be year 2000-compliant but also be sure that their solution is compatible with yours. You need to know that their year 2000 project will be finished early enough for your two companies to thoroughly test the compatibility of your upgraded applications, with time to fix any bugs before Y2K strikes.

You should also consider protecting yourself with a "firewall," special software that runs between your systems and the outside world and prevents certain kinds of data from getting through. Firewalls have traditionally been used to keep out viruses and illicit intruders (hackers), but the same sort of technology can also screen out noncompliant data before it "contaminates" your own. Even if you're quite certain that you won't get noncompliant data from any of your suppliers, you should still consider a firewall because, in this world of rapid change and global accessibility, your staffers could be networking with systems you're not even aware of.

As windowing (having the computer make an educated guess whether a two-digit date is in the twentieth or the twenty-first century) is gaining popularity over field expansion (reprogramming two-digit date fields to four digits), more companies are using windowing in their electronic data interchanges. This requires some coordination, but less than you might think. In an article in the Jan/Feb 1998 issue of *Year/2000 Journal*, Unibol senior consultant Michael Gerner offers a simple suggestion for data interchanges: Prepare a windowing solution, and let your business partner know exactly what "pivot point" you've chosen. (For instance, if "59" is assumed to be 2059, but "60" is assumed to be 1960, then 60 is your pivot point.) "Please note the key point in this approach," he writes. "You are telling your business partners what you are doing. You are not waiting for them to get their act together. You can get away with that in windowing because the date format used in the data does not change. Even if they fix their date problems later than you do, it doesn't matter—they can still read your output and you can still read their input."

This kind of approach may work in some situations. In others, you may require (or be mandated by a governing body) to supply data transfer with four-digit dates. "Expansion bridge" software can do exactly that: transform your windowed dates into four-digit dates for purposes of data transfer, but allow you to work with two-digit dates internally.

IT Suppliers Should Toe the Line

You should be much more stringent in your year 2000 demands when dealing with any companies that provide hardware, software, or materials with embedded computer technology (items that are not computers per se but contain computer chips). In these cases, you have the right to know whether a product is compliant right now, and if not, when it will be replaced with one that is.

External IT suppliers, like all other IT professionals, may not always meet their deadlines, however, so there should be a reasonable margin for error in their plans. If, for instance, they're planning to release a year 2000-compliant upgrade in late 1999, that probably isn't soon enough, and you should proceed on the assumption that the compliant upgrade won't be available in time.

Be aware, too, that just because the new version of a program is announced and certified as year 2000-compliant, this doesn't necessarily mean that it is. Not that software suppliers are dishonest, but when upgrading a program it can be difficult to cover every single usage combination, and some noncompliant data can slip through. So can other types of bugs, accidentally created in the course of a year 2000 upgrade. Keep in mind that your software supplier may be just as pressed for time, and having just as much trouble finding qualified programmers, as you are. So whatever upgrades you receive, you need time to adequately test them before your company begins using them.

Most important, you need to include year 2000 compliance language in all future contracts from now until the year 2000 is safely behind us. The language should plainly state that any new products your hardware or software suppliers deliver from here on are guaranteed to be year 2000-compliant.

If you think this is overkill, then consider this cautionary tale, related by William Ulrich at a year 2000 conference in the summer of 1998 and reported by Jon Huntress of the Year 2000 Information Center (see Recommended Other Reading):

> A chiropractor in a clinic with several other chiropractors knew William was working with the year 2000 problem and asked him a question about the computers he and his fellow chiropractors were planning to buy for their office. The firm was getting a new LAN [local area network] and planned on spending about $80,000. Five vendors were bidding on the package.
>
> The chiropractor wondered if there was anything he should check about the new computers and the year 2000 problem. William told him to ask each vendor specifically if their systems were guaranteed not to have a Y2K problem.
>
> The chiropractor did and found that instead of five vendors, he now only had to deal with two. Three vendors of brand new equipment in early 1998 could not certify an $80,000 package would make the millennium transition just over a year away!
>
> Without William's input the question wouldn't have been asked. How many others in purchasing are making the assumption that if it is new there probably isn't any problem?

Some IT managers report that vendors refuse to include compliance guarantees in their contracts. These issues can certainly lead to difficult negotiations—and it is certainly easier to simply assume that anything being sold today is bound to be compliant. But incidents like the one Ulrich describes are a good illustration of why this is one guarantee you can't afford not to get.

CHAPTER 9

Strategic Decisions

Prudential and the Year 2000

"From the earliest management theories up to contemporary industry research, studies have shown that most project failure results not from technological limitations—but from ineffective project management. This holds especially true for the year 2000 project. Its scope, business risks, and immovable deadline mandate smart and skillful project management."

—IRENE DEC, *YEAR 2000 JOURNAL*, MARCH/APRIL 1998

If you hang around corporate year 2000 project managers and consultants, as I have for most of the last two years, you can't help but hear a lot about Prudential Insurance Company of America and its year 2000 project, considered by many to be the premier model of such an effort.

Prudential has this status for three reasons. First, the company has always treated decisions about the year 2000 as strategic decisions that would affect the company's future. As a result, it put together an incredibly thorough and well-organized Y2K project that has been in place since fall 1995—earlier than most businesses were even aware of the year 2000 problem, let alone taking it seriously enough to do something about it.

The second reason is that the company has made the strategic decision to willingly share extensive information about this effort with its business partners, customers, other year 2000 managers, and the public, in the hopes of helping other organizations manage their Y2K problems and minimizing the glitch's widespread effects.

The third reason is Irene Dec, vice president of corporate information technology, and Prudential's year 2000 program director. She's a woman with a passion for information technology, logical organizational theories and concepts, and untangling year 2000 issues. As well as running Prudential's huge project, Dec writes and speaks regularly on Y2K issues and has achieved such prominence in this field that she recently turned down the offer of a year-long stint as advisor to the special Senate Year 2000 Committee.

Prudential's main lines of business are insurance, health care, investments, securities, employee benefits, real estate, and consumer banking. As an insurance and financial services company, it is very sensitive to the year 2000 problem: The company is highly dependent on computers and electronic data transfer, and a significant amount of what it does is date-sensitive.

At the same time, though, Prudential was in a uniquely good position to recognize the danger early on because it dealt with periods of time reaching years into the future; the company is in the business of assessing risk. Thus, Prudential's is an exception among year 2000 projects, having started early, with full funding (current cost estimates for the completed project are $160 million) and with the full support of the CEO, Art Ryan. "We are committed to making this a nonevent for our customers," Dec explains.

With this in mind, the company began by establishing a set of eight operating principles to guide it through the year 2000 project:

1. Software applications will be repaired or replaced based on rigorous risk and cost analyses.
2. Replacement and contingency plans must be in place by December 31, 1996.
3. Redundant applications performing similar functions will be consolidated where appropriate.
4. Parallel development activities will be carefully researched and assessed to ensure against jeopardizing the timely success of year 2000 maintenance. [In other words, successfully completing this project is a top priority, even if it means putting other IT projects on hold.]

5. All new software will be certified [as year 2000-compliant] before purchase and installation.
6. Standard date formats will be employed in new development. [Prudential has chosen a four-digit year standard.]
7. All applications require year 2000 compliance certification [through Prudential's in-house certification process].
8. All the elements of Prudential's infrastructure [computer hardware, buildings, telecommunications equipment, and even corporate aircraft] require compliance certification.

Although Prudential has seven separate business units, which function independently in many other ways, its entire year 2000 effort is overseen by Dec, who reports directly to the company's CIO, Bill Friel—the kind of central coordination and control that most Y2K experts seem to agree is needed for a project to succeed.

Dec's office is staffed with ten Prudential employees and eight employees of external Y2K consultants. Each of the company's business units also has its own year 2000 office. In all, Dec says, between her office and the Y2K offices at the business units, there are about one hundred Prudential employees at work on the problem. The central project office coordinates a companywide liaison program to help make sure each of the year 2000 offices at the business units meets its objectives.

Thus Dec's staff learns right away if some part of the year 2000 project is falling behind or is at risk. If necessary, the central office can respond by using a "S.W.A.T." team approach, sending troubleshooters to help get the program back on schedule (see Figure 9.1). Dec jokes that, as the year 2000 nears, these team members will be issued Ghostbuster-like jump suits, with "Y2K" emblazoned across the back.

Metrics Matter

No matter how you look at it, when it comes to the year 2000 Prudential is facing a huge challenge. The company has about 80,000 employees, some 140 million lines of code, and exactly 1,118 different computer applications in its portfolio. This last figure typifies Dec's philosophy that any good year 2000 project, large or small, needs to be carefully tracked with comprehensive metrics that give managers a detailed view of exactly how the year 2000 project is advancing.

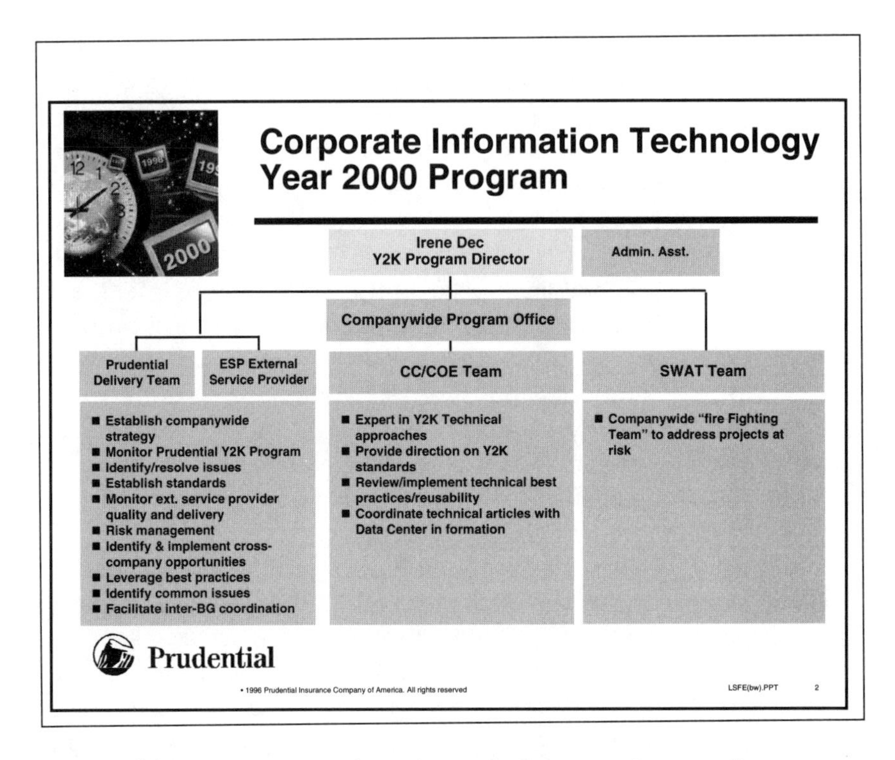

"I'm very metric, data-driven," she says. "I can tell you on a monthly basis where everything in this project is by line of business, where they were supposed to be, where they actually were, and what phase they're in. I can do most of these on a daily basis." You need this kind of precision, she adds, to keep any large year 2000 project on track. "What's absolutely critical for any company to succeed is metrics."

The way Dec deals with these massive amounts of information, and the hugeness of the project itself, is to divide and conquer; she splits everything into more manageable pieces. She has divided the company's year 2000 project itself into three major "chunks":

1. Applications, which includes all software anywhere in the company, whether on a mainframe, client server, or personal computer
2. Infrastructure, which includes such things as the company's buildings and corporate airplane fleet, as well as its PBXs and telecommunications equipment—and the computers themselves

3. External business partners, which deals with, well, its external business partners (see Figure 9.2). From her neatly organized Roseland, N.J., office, she gives me a status report on each.

Figure 9.2: Year 2000 Project Areas

Applications	Infrastructure	External Relationships
Renovate	Vendor software products	Business partners
Replace	Processing environments	Government agencies
Retire	Telecommunications	Suppliers
	Building systems	Customers
	Airfleet	

Eighty-Five Percent Compliant

"We've achieved approximately 85 percent of planned compliance," Dec says. But, she added, for Prudential "compliance" isn't quite good enough. "Prudential has its own certification process," she explains. "A lot of companies don't."

Instead, she says, Prudential uses a fifteen-step certification process in which specific future dates must be tested, with audit review, signatures, and accountability every step of the way. "So when we say we're certified, we really are." By June 30, she adds, about 80 percent of Prudential's internal systems had gone through this certification process and were back in use.

Some of the programs didn't make the deadline because a software supplier failed to supply its compliant version on schedule, or because a program the software company had guaranteed as compliant turned out not to be when given Prudential's rigorous tests. (This is not an uncommon problem, and it reflects not dishonesty on the software company's part but the difficulty of accurately testing the compliance of any software.)

At this writing, most of the software suppliers planned to deliver compliant versions in September 1998. If everything goes as planned, Dec believes that all Prudential applications will be compliant, tested, and certified by the end of December 1998.

For the massive amounts of reprogramming needed in Prudential's own code, the company made the decision early on to have external consultants handle approximately 70 percent of the work. Though Capers Jones's research (see Recommended Other Reading) suggests that keeping such work in house saves on year 2000 repairs, Dec reports finding just the opposite: that taking the work outside would save Prudential big bucks—perhaps as much as $40 million. (One reason for the savings, Dec explains, is that Prudential formed its vendor relationships in mid-1996, before costs escalated.)

But the decision wasn't based on expense; it was another strategic decision: not to tie up its own technical staff during the four years of the project. "Companies that are doing a purely internal fix are making some decisions as to their future development, because you can't have the same technical staff working on new technology and fixing the year 2000 problem," Dec explains. "We did not want to dedicate a lot of our own resources to this project. Prudential is a technology leader now, and we want to be a technology leader in the year 2000."

The PC Problem

Straddling the areas or chunks of infrastructure and applications are the tens of thousands of personal computers in use by Prudential employees. For Dec, this represented a special challenge because it meant going "outside the IT community," from the tightly controlled world of mainframe and client-server applications to the company at large.

Dec tackled the problem by beginning with a very simple question: How many of these are there? She quickly discovered that a complete company inventory of all personal computers did not exist, so she set about looking for ways to create one. It would include all of Prudential's desktops and laptops, and also computers used at home for Prudential work.

Prudential is using a special software tool that can assess the compliance of all these computers and the software installed on them. "I always knew that you could have just gone through your box and tested it and said, 'Yes, this very minute it's compliant,' but seven minutes later someone could load something on it that's not. So I said, 'Why do it?' But then Prudential found this tool, and it produces daily reports, which tell you when new software is loaded."

But even after the computers themselves and the software on them has been certified compliant, Dec says, there's still one more possible danger for personal computers: databases, programs, and spreadsheets that the users themselves have created.

"You have a spreadsheet program, and I can prove it's year 2K-compliant as a version. But did you know you can still go in there and create a spreadsheet that has a two-position year?" Dec says.

Rather than address this worry with every computer user at Prudential, Dec is conducting a project now to find out which of the desktops are used by "critical" users, working with sensitive data that could pose a serious risk if the data aren't right. "We're going to get a snapshot of these critical users," she says. "In other words, folks like actuaries. Folks like that are in the financial organization. So what we're going to do is look at that group and go in with the tools to assess their spreadsheets and databases. But only for this segment, and I suspect these critical guys will be somewhere between five thousand and eight thousand [in number]."

Will It Work in 2000?

As the applications project nears completion, Dec's staff is directing its efforts to the two remaining parts of the project, infrastructure and external business partners. The infrastructure chunk encompasses all the company's computers, as well as its telephone equipment, buildings, corporate jets, and helicopter.* In short, every physical object that could possibly be affected by the year 2000 problem. Here too, Dec says, she has a certification process in place for each of these items.

When it comes to certifying Prudential's buildings, the company has been doing its own tests, year 2000 dates during weekends to make sure heat, air conditioning, and elevators work properly.

High Risk or Low Risk?

"We realized that unless our partners are Y2K capable and can play in this Y2K game, even though we took care of applications and infrastructure, we were at risk," Dec notes. "So in late summer 1997, we put a strategy together on how we're going to handle external partners."

External partners, she explains, include both business partners and suppliers. Business partners are, for example, the banks and financial institutions Prudential works with, and the HMO partners in its health care business. Suppliers include, say, trucking firms that fulfill Prudential's needs in its relocation business, and also utilities. (For details on how Y2K can affect utilities, see Chapter Thirteen.)

As with the other two areas of the project, Dec's first step was to inventory suppliers; she discovered there were more than one thousand. Her next step was to split the group into critical and noncritical suppliers, much as she did with personal computer users. She wound up with about 280 in the most critical category. In the next phase, she says, her staff focused on these most-critical users and conducted a risk assessment. It began by sending out a survey to determine how serious these users were about the year 2000 problem.

What kind of questions were on the survey? Dec reports that questions such as: *Is this project considered the number one project in your company? In the top five? In the top ten? In the top fifty?* "Instead of just asking, 'Is there executive commitment?'—everyone's going to say yes—you can tag it as to what level." *Do you do reporting and metrics? And is that done quarterly? Monthly? As needed?* "That tells you a lot. Then it asks, *Do you have metrics that compare the planned date to actual?*"

Perhaps because they were sent out in the summer of 1997, before the real deluge of such inquiries had begun, Prudential got a 70 percent return rate on this survey. Based on the answers (or lack thereof), Dec's staff divided these critical suppliers into high-risk and low-risk categories. Those who did not return the survey were given two follow-up calls; if they persisted in not responding they were assumed to be high-risk.

In the next phase, Prudential assembled a risk assessment team (or RAT) for each of its lines of business. The RAT included members from legal, audit, integrated control, the business's management, and the year 2000 program manager for that line of business. These teams created a profile of all Prudential partners, determining both the level and the type of risk (risk to revenues, to reputation, or to customers, for example) each represented.

The last phase, Dec says, is contingency planning, something Prudential takes quite seriously. For instance, in a place where the local power utility is both critical and high-risk, she has insisted on having generators on site by December 1, 1999. Waiting till the power goes out to bring in generators is a bad idea, she says, because "if we're going to need electricity, so is everyone else in that area." If the power stays on, she adds, the generators can eventually be returned. "That's not heightened behavior; we consider that smart behavior," she says. "We call it 'business continuation.'"

Trading Surveys

How does Prudential deal with the surveys it receives? "As soon as I saw the potential, I saw that we were going to have a lot of these," Dec relates. "And when you have a lot of anything, you want to have a process and methodology in place. Then you can respond quickly."

By now, it should be no surprise to hear that the first step of this methodology was to divide these inquiries into three categories: government agencies (both domestic and international), customers, and business partners. For each, year 2000 staff have created a standard response that could be sent along with whatever survey needed to be completed. Because of Prudential's decision to share a great deal of information, these are sometimes thick packages, she says. The company decided to send some of these out proactively; for instance, after a few requests from state governments, the government package was sent to all fifty states.

Dec also put together a system for tracking these requests and was thus able to tell me, for example, that though the company had received only 171 of them for all of 1997, by mid-July 1998 it had already gotten 1,170 more, with the numbers increasing every month. "It's just constantly going up," Dec says. Whenever a year 2000 inquiry comes in anywhere in the company, Prudential employees know they must report the inquiry to the Y2K staff, which then takes care of responding.

A Common Threat

Prudential's willingness to share lots of information, and take all the time needed to fill out year 2000 surveys, reflects another strategic decision: that cooperation and information sharing among companies is the only logical way to face this threat. Prudential has, in some cases, shared the cost of year 2000 repairs with external partners who could not have afforded them otherwise.

In the end, Dec believes, this kind of commitment to partnering means stronger relationships than ever before. And there's a bigger picture here, she feels. "I happen to believe that, if you look at it, the world is faced with an issue. The world has never really had a common problem to share before, where every country and every business in the world has a common problem—and the key is working together to solve it."

CHAPTER 10

So You Think You're Too Small to Worry About 2000?

"A recent Wells Fargo bank survey shows that of the small businesses that even know about the problem, roughly half intend to do nothing about it. Now, this is not one of the summer movies where you can close your eyes during the scary parts. Every business, of every size, with eyes wide open, must face the future and act."

—PRESIDENT BILL CLINTON, IN A SPEECH TO THE NATIONAL ACADEMY OF SCIENCES, JULY 14, 1998 (HIS FIRST SPEECH DEVOTED TO THE YEAR 2000 PROBLEM)

To face the year 2000 without fear, large and medium-sized companies with huge mainframes or client-server systems need large, well-funded, well-managed year 2000 projects, complete with CEO commitment. But what about small companies, home offices, or even individuals who depend on computers for some part of their work or personal lives?

Most seem to be simply ignoring the year 2000 problem, in the hope that it will go away by itself. Recently, I talked with Norbert Kubilus, a consultant and software expert who has worked on Y2K projects with a variety of small businesses (defined as those with revenues of less than $5 million a year), ranging in size from three to one hundred people. The lack of preparedness he's found is astonishing. "Maybe one out of five is unaware, or barely aware, of the problem," he says. Perhaps two out of five actually plan on doing something about the problem—sometime in 1999.

"One fellow I talked with has a small manufacturing operation," Kubilus adds. " There is the potential for what he manufactures to go directly into the trash heap. Small business owners just don't recognize the different problems that can arise."

Worse, a lot of small business managers are counting on someone else to solve the year 2000 problem for them. They believe that either some software genius will come up with an all-powerful silver bullet to fix the millennium glitch everywhere, or at least their own software and hardware suppliers will deal with Y2K for them. "Overoptimism about suppliers and vendors is pandemic among small businesses," Kubilus notes.

The danger is especially acute, he adds, because most small businesses cannot survive even a brief interruption: "When a small business is shut down for more than five days by any kind of disaster, history shows that there's an 80 percent chance that company will be out of business within a year."

Because small businesses are less likely to be computerized—and more likely to have simple computer systems if they are—Capers Jones predicts in his book that small businesses face only a 3 percent chance of failure on account of year 2000 problems. This is much less than the 5–7 percent chance of failure he sees for mid-size firms, which Jones defines as one thousand to ten thousand employees.

Of course, Jones notes, small businesses very frequently fail for reasons that have nothing to do with the year 2000 problem, so the 3 percent risk should be seen as an add-on to the tremendous risk of failure most small businesses are already facing. Which, in fact, puts the problem in a nutshell: Many small business managers can't take the time to tackle Y2K because they are too busy dealing with what seem to be more immediate threats. As always, the year 2000 problem is mostly one of priorities.

Jones notwithstanding, I believe small businesses face some special year 2000 challenges, among them:

1. *"Shrink-wrapped" software.* Small businesses are much less likely than their larger counterparts to have custom-written code, and much more likely to depend on off-the-shelf software products for their essential business functions. Obviously, this is a huge advantage; it

means you're not responsible for fixing your own software. On the other hand . . . *someone else* is responsible for fixing your own software. Depending on what degree of help they offer, this can also be a distinct disadvantage.

2 *Embedded chips.* All businesses, large and small, need to be concerned about embedded chips in electronic devices other than computers. But small businesses may have greater reason to worry because they are likelier than big businesses to be dealing with electronic equipment bought from a third party, or bought used. A business that has, for instance, inherited its phone system from a previous tenant may have a hard time finding out whether that system is year 2000-compliant.

It could, of course, contact the manufacturer—but the manufacturer is likely to be equally uninformed. Since the equipment was mostly likely sold through a third party and may have changed hands several times before the current business acquired it, the manufacturer probably has no idea whether the device is using a newer, compliant version of its operating software or an older, noncompliant one. This leaves the small business with an unpleasant choice: Either replace the equipment (assuming it has enough cash on hand to do so) or wait until the year 2000 and find out the hard way whether the equipment works or not.

Now imagine this same scenario played out with security doors (which often lock and unlock according to the date), copiers, fax machines, factory equipment, and time-card punching machines—to name just a few possible trouble spots.

3 *Getting help.* Even assuming there are still some outside consultants available to help manage corporate year 2000 projects when this book appears, it seems likely they'll be able to pick and choose their clients. In that situation, a small business, lacking both the deep pockets and high-prestige reputation of a larger organization, is likely to find itself at the back of the line. The same may hold true if the business decides to try to hire its own year 2000 project manager.

4 *Finances.* Many small businesses lack cash under the best of circumstances, and the year 2000 is likely to be the worst of circumstances. Dealing with Y2K may be expensive, but not dealing with it is not an option. The year 2000 might threaten your operations, but it also affects your ability to borrow money because most banks now include an assessment of year 2000 readiness when considering a business loan.

5 *Shipping.* Anyone who lived through the 1997 UPS strike knows that shipping is an essential link in the business chain for many small businesses. In Chapter Thirteen, I explain in more detail why I think shipping is particularly vulnerable to the year 2000 problem. If I'm right and there's a shipping squeeze, who do you think shipping companies will serve first: the largest companies that ship millions of packages a year, or a small company that may only send a few hundred?

6 *Competition for essential supplies.* This may be the biggest Y2K threat to small businesses. If the year 2000 causes disruption in the manufacturing and shipping industries, then the same demand for goods and services will find itself chasing a substantially decreased supply.

In other words, imagine you're a small shirt manufacturer. You import the buttons for your shirts from Thailand, via a company that supplies not only you but half the garment manufacturers in your state.

Now the year 2000 hits and suddenly this button manufacturer finds it either cannot produce or cannot ship as many buttons as it has orders for. Only 60 percent of the planned shipment makes it to your area. In this case, too, the company's largest customers are likeliest to get high priority, and you might find yourself switching to zippers.

So What Do I Do About It?

One reason small-business owners are failing to act is that they aren't sure what to do. In a larger organization, one would normally appoint a single person with ultimate responsibility for the year 2000 project's success. In a small business, which probably doesn't have an information technology staff, and sometimes not even an on-staff technology person, this may not be a practical step.

In the absence of someone to take on the year 2000 as a project, the next best step is for small business owners to prepare themselves by learning as much as possible about it. One good place to do this is the special Small Business Administration Web page on the subject, http://www.sba.gov/y2k. Another is Prudential's Web page, http://www.prudential.com, where you can download a whole package of year 2000 information that Irene Dec has assembled expressly for small businesses. It includes forms to fill out to help you evaluate every step of your year 2000 project.

It is, admittedly, difficult for most small business executives to spend a lot of time learning about this complex issue. To make matters worse, once you do, it may still be quite difficult to decide which course of action you need to take. But don't let the difficulty of the issue scare you away; as always with the year 2000, your worst choice is to do nothing.

The Personal Computer Problem

What if you, like me, are utterly dependent on a single personal computer? Thousands of individual users and people with home offices across the country count on their PCs to work properly, and over the past year or so hundreds of articles have appeared instructing people how to Y2K-proof their own computers. Unfortunately, things are often not as simple as these articles make them seem.

The rule of thumb for PC hardware and software is, basically, the newer it is, the likelier it is to be year 2000-compliant. But that doesn't mean people with newer computers have nothing to worry about. Karl Feilder, president of Greenwich Mean Time, a well-known PC hardware and software testing firm, says that according to his tests 93 percent of PCs manufactured before 1997 are not year 2000-compliant. Forty-seven percent of those made in the first six months of 1997 failed the test, as did 21 percent of those built in the second half of 1997. Things are getting better, but they're not fixed yet; 11 percent of the 1998 PCs he's tested still flunked.

Of course it should go without saying that any new computer or computer product you buy from here on in should come with a written year 2000 guarantee. (Be aware of this issue, also, if you're one of the many people who download freeware or shareware from the Internet.)

If, on the other hand, you're one of those who like to hang on to old technology for as long as possible, and you're still clinging to hardware and software that dates from the 1980s, then you're pretty much guaranteed to have a year 2000 problem.

How can you find out if the product you're using is compliant? Not easily, I'm sorry to say. Unfortunately, there isn't any straightforward way for a layperson to test year 2000 compliance. "Nobody has come up with a simple test most anybody can use," Kubilus says.

If this seems odd to you, keep in mind that it's not uncommon for a software manufacturer to claim that a certain piece of software is compliant, only to discover through rigorous testing by customers or other professionals that it isn't. The reason for this is not deceptiveness or stupidity on the part of the software maker. Rather, it's an indication of how difficult it is to create a test thorough enough to catch every possible manifestation of the year 2000 glitch. If professionals can't do it, chances are home computer users can't do it either.

How likely is your PC to be affected by the year 2000? Technology columnist Virginia Baldwin Hick put the situation succinctly: "The answer to virtually any question about hardware or software Y2K vulnerability is, 'It depends.'"[1]

To make matters more complicated, there are four different levels at which a personal computer could potentially be affected by the year 2000 problem.

BIOS

Short for basic input output system (but there's absolutely no reason why you need to know that), BIOS is a bit of software that is hard-wired into your computer and controls how its internal clock tells time. Whether your BIOS is year 2000-ready is probably the first question you should ask yourself in relation to the year 2000 and your PC, because if BIOS isn't functioning properly, everything you do on your computer is at risk.

Fortunately, BIOS may be the one area of PC vulnerability that you can adequately test by yourself. Several software experts have proposed the following simple test: First back up any material on your computer that you would be sorry to lose. (Don't blame me if you decide to skip this step and regret it later!) Then manually set your computer to a few minutes before midnight, December 31, 1999, and watch and see if it rolls over correctly. If that goes well, reset the computer to just before midnight a second time, and then turn it off. Go away for a few minutes and then turn the computer back on to see if it accurately rolls over while off.

Hick, on the other hand, recommends against this procedure. Your PC has both a real-time clock and a virtual clock, and you may end up testing one without testing the other. Worse, she claims, you could wind up damaging software that's already on your hard drive. Instead, she recommends downloading a free test from the NSTL Website, and running that. The site is at http://www.nstl.com.

Whichever test you choose, if you do have a problem it's probably not the end of the world. Assuming your machine is reasonably new, you should be able to get a new, improved version of BIOS, and perhaps a new real-time clock, from your computer's manufacturer.

Operating System

If you're one of those hardy souls still clinging to Windows 3.1 or some earlier version of Windows, or even MS-DOS, now might be the time to consider a change, since these are known not to be year 2000-compliant. For later versions, the situation is somewhat unclear. A few months ago, Microsoft was confidently declaring that Windows 95, Windows 98, and Windows NT were all Y2K-compliant. Since then, they've failed some user tests (once again demonstrating the difficulty of accurate Y2K testing), and Microsoft has had to adjust its claims to be "compliant with minor issues."

I can only suggest that you check Microsoft's Website (http://www.microsoft.com) for the latest information. Incidentally, if you're not sure whether your computer's BIOS is compliant, you should be aware that the more recent Windows operating systems may actually compensate for a noncompliant BIOS—during the year 2000. It's therefore quite possible for a computer that seems to be working perfectly to glitch in the year *2001*.

As far as Apple computers are concerned, the Mac OS (operating system) seems to be compliant. Apple appears to have addressed the year 2000 problem well ahead of its competitors, and many Mac users are smugly rejoicing that they have nothing at all to worry about.

Is this true? Not quite. Having hardware and an operating system that is year 2000-ready is a great start, but it's only a start because no one uses an operating system alone.

Applications

Computer users (including Mac users) typically have a large number of programs installed on their PCs at any given time. These software applications are all potentially vulnerable to the year 2000 problem, and you should check the Y2K status of any you really depend on. For instance, Microsoft has admitted that there are some year 2000 problems in its Office suite.

How can you check the status of an individual application? You can set the dates forward and play around with it, setting it, for instance, to February 29, 2000. (The year 2000 is a leap year, but many computer programs don't know that.) It's a good idea to do this, but ultimately you probably need to check with the manufacturer to find out the product's year 2000 status. If you're told that the version you have is definitely compliant, then you're probably fine, though it's wise to stay on the alert, since new year 2000 glitches are being discovered all the time.

It's particularly important to be aware of the potential for year 2000 trouble when dealing with spreadsheet or financial software of any kind, since errors in these kinds of programs can have catastrophic results. Indeed, Ian Hayes has officially predicted that the worst year 2000 disaster will result from a bad decision made with information from a noncompliant spreadsheet. To make matters worse, many applications of this type have relatively recent versions out that are not year 2000-ready.

What happens if you do discover that you have a problem? Then, as they say, the plot thickens. At this writing, some software companies are offering free upgrades or "patches" to recent versions of software that turn out to be noncompliant. Meanwhile, many others are requiring that users buy a new, improved, upgraded and, incidentally, compliant version of the software instead. This requirement has prompted a lot of ill will and several class-action lawsuits from computer users who claim that they're entitled to software that will continue to work in the year 2000 without having to pay extra for an upgrade. Until recently, Intuit was facing not one but two such class-action suits over its popular online banking program Quicken (a conflict I discussed more fully in Chapter Six).

The only decision that's been rendered so far favored the defendant. But if plaintiffs have significant wins in the future, it may become normal practice for software companies to offer free year 2000 upgrades to PC users.

Your Own Creations

Even though your computer, operating system, and applications are all perfectly year 2000-compliant, you could still wind up running afoul of Y2K. If you're the sort of sophisticated user who has written a few simple programs for your own use, or created databases or spreadsheets of your own using two-digit instead of four-digit years, then you have inadvertently produced your very own year 2000 problem.

If this is the case, of course, you wrote it, so presumably you understand it. Thus it's up to you to fix it yourself. Also, you should never say another unkind word about all those foolish programmers who lacked the foresight to use four-digit dates!

Note

1. Virginia Baldwin, "Here's How to Test Your Computer for the Year 2000 Bug," *St. Louis Post-Dispatch* (July 20,1998).

CHAPTER 11

Embedded Chips

Buried Problems

"Chances are if you have voice mail, a cellular phone, a fax, or a copier, you're going to experience some type of year 2000 glitch related to the embedded processors. We just don't know where all these processors are and which ones are going to fail."

—MICHAEL HARDEN, PRESIDENT, CENTURY TECHNOLOGY SERVICES

Imagine that every piece of equipment you use, from your car to your copier to your phone system to your fax machine, had a tiny device inside of it that you could neither see nor reach, and that this device might—or might not—allow the equipment to work properly after December 31, 1999. Now, imagine that these devices exist not only in your bits of equipment, but also in the elevator that gets you to your office, the heating and cooling systems for your building, the doors to your business, and even the companies that deliver electricity to your facility.

Worried yet? You can stop imagining, because it's true. Computer chips (also called "programmable logic calculators" or PLCs) are embedded inside a staggering array of electronic and mechanical devices, and inside many things, such as air conditioning systems and security doors, that we don't traditionally think of as "machines" at all. This is why many year 2000 experts I've talked to believe that the Y2K software problem—for all its threats—is relatively trivial, that the *real* year 2000 disaster will come from embedded chip failures.

"People don't talk about embedded chips that much," observed an acquaintance of mine who's working on Y2K for his organization. He's right, they don't—because embedded chips present a pernicious problem to which there is no obvious solution. Unlike a computer, a chip cannot be reprogrammed. Most can't be tested either, so there's no certain way to know whether a chip is year 2000-compliant or not. The only sure way to eliminate the problem is to replace either the chip or the entire device containing the chip. Consider that these devices include things like oil drilling equipment deep in the ocean floor, or satellites, or bank vault doors, or airplanes, and you begin to see the scope of the problem.

Two Percent of 25 Billion Equals 500 Million

Are most chips likely to be date-sensitive? Absolutely not. The highest estimate I've ever heard is that 30 percent of chips might be non-year 2000-compliant (this estimate was in a manufacturing context), and the lowest I've heard is that only 2 percent might be noncompliant. The problem is that by the year 2000, there will an estimated 25 billion devices containing computer chips in use around the world and—well, as you can see from the heading of this section, I've already done the math for you.

Where are embedded chips likely to cause the most trouble? Take a good look at the following:

- Any electronic office equipment (sophisticated copiers, faxes, etc.)
- In-house phone systems or equipment
- Company cars or trucks
- Corporate planes
- Any medical equipment you or your staff depend on

- Bar code readers and other such devices
- Heating/ventilation/air conditioning systems
- Elevator systems
- Any automatically locking and unlocking security doors

This last category is very high-risk. I've heard of so many problems involving security doors I tend to think anyone that has one should check it for year 2000 compliance immediately. For instance, consider one 24-hour convenience store chain I know. Now, there's a company that you might think would have no security door problem—after all, under normal circumstances, their doors never close, so one would think there'd be no earthly reason that a set of doors should be date-sensitive. But it is, automatically locking on one day a year—Christmas day. If the year 2000 manager who told me this story hadn't noticed the problem, his company's stores would have locked at midnight on New Year's Eve, 1999—trapping whoever was there inside.

A story, probably apocryphal, is worth sharing here:

> A bank wanted the safest vault in the world, so it embedded the controller chip deep in the door of the vault. For even better security, the vault was set in place first, and the walls of the bank were built around it. Nobody was going to get into that vault!
>
> The problem is that the vault was automatically set to open on weekdays and lock on weekends. Unfortunately, January 1, 2000, will be a Saturday, while January 1, 1900 (to which the vault is likely to revert because it isn't year 2000-compliant) was a Monday. Thus, the vault will be unlocked for the first Saturday and Sunday of the year 2000 (because the door will believe these days are actually Monday and Tuesday), will remain open Monday, Tuesday, and Wednesday of the following week, believing they are Wednesday, Thursday, and Friday, and then lock tight on Thursday

> and Friday of the following week, cutting off depositors' access to their money. The only solution is to demolish the bank.

An Embedded Chip Action Plan

"OK," you say, "I'm concerned about embedded chips. So what do I do about them?"

The first step is to find out exactly how many of these things you have in your company. This will be quite a bit harder than getting an accurate count of your company's hardware and software, but if you don't start out knowing what you're dealing with you'll have no way to know whether you've solved the problem or not.

I've encountered many differing opinions from year 2000 experts on how easy or difficult it might be to tell whether a piece of equipment contains a computer chip, and whether that chip is date-sensitive. Ultimately, you probably need a technical expert to do this, since even engineers have sometimes been surprised to discover which devices among those they worked with contain chips.

But in the May/June 1998 issue of the *Year/2000 Journal*, year 2000 expert Dave Bettinger offers some good basic guidelines that can help you make an educated guess as to which devices are likely to have a year 2000 problem. He argues that to be affected by Y2K, an electronic device must have both an internal power pack or battery (because devices without them cannot keep track of the date or time when they are turned off) and the ability to display a date.

Note that I said the ability to display a date, not a display. Many devices that don't have a display of their own can still display a date (along with a lot of other information) if they are hooked up to a diagnostic device. This is the kind of reason why you need someone with some technical expertise to make the final determination.

Combine this information with your in-house analysis of which devices are "mission-critical" (that is, if they don't work right it can have an impact on your company's survival) to determine which devices get the most immediate attention; as with computers and software, there's a good chance you may not have time to evaluate every device.

Once you've inventoried and prioritized your equipment, what should your next step be? Most electronic devices cannot be easily tested for year 2000 vulnerability, but it's probably a good idea to test whatever you can, by setting the date to a few dates in the year 2000, including February 29. (Make sure you have a backup device on hand, on the off chance that a tested device may stop working permanently.)

But such testing is just an interim step that only works with certain devices and may not guarantee proper year 2000 performance. Your most important step is to contact each device's manufacturer, and ask whether it contains a noncompliant chip or not.

The problem is, the manufacturers themselves may not know. Recently, I heard about a company that had several devices (I don't remember what they were) of the same make and model number from a single manufacturer. When contacted, the manufacturer offered assurances that the devices were year 2000-compliant, but the company's Y2K manager, being extremely thorough, insisted on testing the devices anyway. All of them.

It turned out to be a very good thing. Some of them turned out to be compliant, others not. What gives? the company asked the manufacturer. The manufacturer didn't know either, until it did some research into its own manufacturing processes and discovered that the same products had been built with chips from two different batches, and the batches came from two different chip suppliers!

The moral is simple: The potential for mistakes, misunderstandings, and incorrect information on this subject is virtually unlimited. What should you do? One recourse is to go to an independent source for product information—but make sure the information results from their own testing, not manufacturers' compliance statements.

Another worthwhile step is to make manufacturers legally responsible by having them certify the product's compliance. Depending on what promises they've made, their degree of confidence in their product, and the nature of your relationship, it may or may not be an easy matter to get manufacturers to agree to such certification. But at the very least, they should certainly provide it for any new purchases.

Embedded Chips Trip Up Manufacturing

Nowhere is the embedded chip problem more troublesome than in manufacturing, where chips control everything from robotics to bar code readers to enormous smelting vats. Date readers can cause real trouble if they fail to correctly interpret expiration dates. One plant reported finding that 10 percent of its chips were non-year 2000-compliant, but that these 10 percent would affect 50 percent of its systems if not remediated in time. Similar potential for trouble has been reported by other manufacturing facilities as well.

To make matters worse, in some cases, IT specialists who may be managing an effective year 2000 project as far as computers and software are concerned have simply not considered the issue of embedded chips in factory equipment because it's outside their traditional bailiwick—leaving those companies with the unappealing possibility that their computers will work perfectly in the year 2000, while the factory itself shuts down.

For manufacturing companies—especially those that are getting a late start—Cargill, a primarily agricultural company with 922 plants around the world, offers an intriguing alternative to the usual top-down, highly structured year 2000 project. This strategy was presented at a recent Y2K conference. Cargill is very decentralized, with many decisions made right on the factory floor, and its employees are accustomed to a great deal of autonomy, so it made sense to the company to give each plant responsibility for dealing with Y2K.

Cargill's plan includes factory walk-throughs at six-month intervals, in which suspect parts are identified and catalogued. This needs to be done by an electrician or an engineer, along with a couple of people who are familiar with the plant. (The cornerstone of this philosophy is that the people who work in the plant are most familiar with the equipment and best know how to deal with it.)

Using Websites or corporate intranets, the different plants or different functions within a plant can all trade information on best practices, solutions, and problems to watch out for. For all important pieces of equipment, a workaround that allows the machine to keep functioning (such as setting the calendar back eight years) is identified, and instructions for the workaround are posted on the machine itself, so anyone on hand can get things running again in case of a stoppage. With these precautions in place, Cargill feels safe using a wait-and-see approach with non-critical systems.

For systems that the Cargill folks can't fix or circumvent, or those created by manufacturers that aren't around anymore, Cargill can and will call in outside year 2000 vendors, but only to deal with the specific situation or piece of equipment. That way, the company doesn't need to lose time teaching a vendor how the particular company's plants operate, something that is almost always necessary in a manufacturing setting. But ultimately, responsibility for preventing Y2K disasters rests with the people at the plant itself.

Many year 2000 professionals question the validity of Cargill's approach, which goes against the conventional wisdom that a year 2000 project should have one person responsible for all fixes and should be managed in a centralized way. Admittedly, the plan is unlikely to work in a very large plant, or in a company that does not traditionally give its plant staff this kind of autonomy. In these situations, a traditional, centralized, and tightly managed year 2000 project is the only viable option. But for the growing number of plants that do have decentralized management, it's an option that might make it possible to deal with the year 2000 problem a little more quickly and effectively.

Whichever plan you use, the important thing for anyone in manufacturing is to get the year 2000 problem well on its way to being remediated as quickly as possible. Most factories today are highly computerized, finely tuned systems where a slight glitch can stop production or cause components to pile up unused. These factories are stunningly efficient, but they can also be very vulnerable. A handful of year 2000 malfunctions, if they occur in the right places, could be enough to bring everything to a grinding halt.

CHAPTER 12

Banking on 2000

"1999 will not be a year of innovation. We want to make sure that all details are buttoned down and we're ready for 2000."

—JAMES P. MCDONOUGH, PRESIDENT AND CEO, ABINGDON SAVINGS BANK

You write a check on your corporate bank account. The money's there—or at least you expect it to be—but the bank hasn't been making deposits into your account on schedule. Or worse: Your account and all information about it have vanished into thin air.

Most of us are so dependent on banks to work accurately and dependably that a world in which we cannot, well, bank on them is just about unimaginable. When it comes to banking, there's good news and bad news. The bad news is that banks—highly computerized, dealing with massive amounts of data daily, and deeply interdependent—are extremely vulnerable to the year 2000 problem. The good news is, they've been aware of it longer than most other industries and are better prepared than most.

So I believe that, although there may be glitches and inconveniences, there will be no major disasters in the banking and financial industries because of the year 2000—although I know some other Y2K experts may disagree with me about this.

Not that the threat isn't real. In testimony before the Senate field hearing on "The Implications of the Year 2000 Computer

Problem" held in early 1998,[1] David M. Iacino, senior manager of the millennium project for BankBoston, described some of what could have happened if the bank had not corrected its year 2000 malfunctions:

> We would not have been able to mature our customers' certificates of deposits in the year 2000 and beyond;
>
> Our negotiable collateral system would have lost expiration dates and review dates on collateral used to secure loans in the event of loan default;
>
> The system processing our daily volume of $800 million of controlled disbursements for our corporate customers would have been inoperable for ten days while the problem was corrected in January 2000, resulting in massive overdrafts to the bank.

Certainly, these would all have been serious problems. But it's important to note that they had all been found and corrected by early 1998. BankBoston, like Prudential, began its year 2000 project in 1995, early enough to get a good solid grip on the worst aspects of the problem. Of course, BankBoston's year 2000 project is no more typical of such efforts than Prudential's is; both have been held up as examples of how these things should be done. But it is fair to say that most banks and financial institutions are ahead of most other industries.

When Donna Tanoue became the new head of the Federal Deposit Insurance Corporation, I was heartened to note that she stated from the beginning that dealing with Y2K would be her first priority. As I've said elsewhere, the year 2000 problem now seems to me to be one of priorities. There was a time when government and business leaders tended to treat the problem as a joke, but it's been many months since anyone dared laugh at Y2K. At this writing, the crucial question seems to be whether people are willing to set this problem ahead of all others, as James McDonough does in the quote that begins this chapter. So to hear the new head of the agency that insures the bank accounts of ordinary citizens call the year 2000 the top priority was very heartening. Here is one industry, at least, that is likely to take the year 2000 seriously.

Cease and Desist!

It's difficult to imagine that, as early as the fall of 1997—when Y2K still was a joke in many people's minds—a government agency would take the step of shutting down a business because of its lack of year 2000 readiness. But the FDIC stopped just short of doing precisely that.

In November 1997, the FDIC, along with the Federal Reserve and the Georgia Department of Banking, issued a cease-and-desist order to Putnam-Greene Financial, Corp., a chain of three banks with assets of about $200 million, based in Eatonton, Georgia. Putnam-Greene was singled out because its computer system was obviously inadequate; balances were not updated for an entire week because of a (non-Y2K) malfunction. But once investigators looked into Putnam-Greene's systems, they flagged its failure to prepare for the year 2000 as a major cause for concern. The cease-and-desist order is one of the harshest warnings banking regulators can issue before actually levying penalties.

The message was clear. "If you were on a board of directors of a bank, you would have to be brain-dead at this point not to realize the regulators are very much concerned about this issue," H. Rogdin Cohen, a banking lawyer with the New York firm Sullivan & Cromwell told the *New York Times* at the time of the order.[2] He further speculated that small banks unable to afford to bring their computer systems up to year 2000 compliance might decide instead that it was a good time to sell.

Indeed, small banks are having a harder time dealing with the year 2000 than their larger counterparts are. At the time of the cease-and-desist order, a Gartner Group study had just reported that only 30 percent of the nation's small banks were at least a quarter of the way through their Y2K projects, as opposed to 90 percent of larger banks.

Cohen's prediction appears to be coming true. The wave of banking mergers that we've seen over the last year and a half is mostly just what it appears to be: consolidation in an industry that favors the large over the small. But Y2K has been lurking under the surface as a motivator in some of these mergers for exactly the reasons Cohen observed, namely, many smaller banks can't afford the help they need to deal with the year 2000 problem. Although other small or medium-sized businesses might be tempted to wait and see whether the uncorrected bug really does force them to close their doors, banking regulators have made it clear that they will not allow that to happen in this industry.

Early in 1998, CoreState Bank in Philadelphia became the first institution to openly admit that it had opted to sell rather than face the millennium bug alone. When asked at the bank's final shareholders' meeting whether Y2K had been a factor in its decision to sell to rival First Union, departing CEO Terry Larsen answered that the problem was a "key thing" in his decision. CoreState faced "substantial exposure and risk," he added, because the bank's computer systems, patched together over years of making acquisitions of its own, would be difficult to bring into compliance in time.[3]

"We Can Do It With Typewriters!"

Of those banks that do plan to deal with the year 2000 problem, many are taking the issue much more seriously than their counterparts in other industries. For instance, even though banking today is so highly computerized it would be difficult to imagine a bank doing business manually, many are making preparations to do exactly that, having noted that even if their own computers are running properly, local power outages are a real possibility. Some banks are preparing themselves by planning a day of manual transactions as a test run before the year 2000 actually hits. Others are arming themselves with extra generators and backup security. Some are stocking manual typewriters and handheld calculators, just in case.

Another way banks are preparing for Y2K is by carefully evaluating their loan applicants for year 2000 readiness. "Credit policy is being reviewed to account for the potential risk that the borrower's ability to repay outstanding debt may be affected by the impact of the year 2000 on the borrower," noted BankBoston's Iacino in his Senate testimony. "Increased allowances for potential loan losses are accordingly being evaluated. Existing loans requiring customer unqualified financial statements are being watched in the event that the customer's own millennium preparation expense may erode comfortable profit margins."

The message is clear: Banks fear that a rash of year 2000-related failures among borrowers could threaten their own financial health. Corporate credit seekers now report that year 2000 assessment is a routine part of loan evaluation.

Meanwhile, the FDIC is continuing its efforts. It has set the end of 1998 as a deadline for banks to be year 2000-ready, and ready for industrywide testing. Also, at this writing the agency has recently completed a series of onsite year 2000 evaluations at insured banks, although FDIC rules prohibit the banks in question from disclosing the ratings they received (they are also prohibited from disclosing FDIC ratings on other matters, such as financial health).

If any banks are foolhardy enough to persist in ignoring the year 2000 problem, the FDIC is preparing to shut them down on the basis of "technological insolvency." The idea is to allow the FDIC to take over these institutions just as many financially insolvent institutions were taken over during the savings and loan crisis. This needs some careful rethinking of current rules, and FDIC lawyers are currently trying to draft a legal definition for technological insolvency. As one FDIC official notes, there are few if any legal precedents for taking over a bank on technological grounds.

Nothing to Fear But Fear Itself

Ironically, the greatest year 2000 threat to banks does not come from their own computer systems, vendor software, or even the possibility of a power outage at their local utilities. The most dangerous aspect of the year 2000 for many banks is their customers, or more specifically, how those customers might react to Y2K.

I've been interviewed about the year 2000 many times in the past few months, and the question of whether banks can be trusted is one that comes up almost every time. "Should I take all my money out of the bank?" is often the question, or even the declarative: "I'm going to take all my money out of the bank." People who have never for a moment considered what would happen if a year 2000 glitch tripped up their local utility, local grocery store, or local hospital have been worrying for a long time about what to do with their money, even though it's insured by the FDIC.

The danger of course, is a series of runs on banks straight out of the Depression, and the lack of confidence that ensues if banks are forced to begin rationing cash. Banks, of course, typically keep less than 10 percent of their assets on hand in cash form, so they are very vulnerable to this kind of panic.

Even without a run on the banks per se, there's a danger of a serious cash shortage. Many year 2000 experts, including Ed Yourdon, whose book has become a best-seller, advise laying in some extra cash around the end of 1999—even if it's only enough to get through a few weeks, in case of, say, ATM problems. Highly reasonable, sound advice. There's just one thing: The nation's current cash supply would quickly be exhausted if even a small portion of the population tried to follow it. Fortunately, the Federal Reserve, which seems more alert to year 2000 dangers than many other government agencies, has asked the Treasury to print $50 billion in extra currency, just in case.

Wall Street Sets the Clock Forward

Of less stringent concern to many people is how the financial industry is preparing for the year 2000 problem, but here too the industry appears to be ahead of the Y2K game. As with banking, Wall Street's greatest vulnerability may lie in its interconnectivity and interdependence. A weak link in the transaction chain could cause enormous havoc, so the financial industry made an early priority of testing all these connections.

In fact, the $270 billion securities industry became the first to move beyond testing at individual firms and into testing the links among interconnected companies. In this case, the motivating force was not a government regulator, but the Security Industries Association, which has been warning of the millennium threat from early on.

Results? So far, so good. The test, which was spread over ten days, simulated trades from December 29, 1999, through January 3, 2000, the first Monday after the century rollover. It covered a wide variety of securities, including stocks, options, and corporate and municipal bonds. Minor connection and year 2000 glitches were reported, but overall the organizers were tremendously pleased with the results. "The four-day process showed us that we can successfully simulate trading in a year 2000 environment," according to Donald Kittell, executive vice president of the SIA.[4]

The test included twenty-nine brokerage firms, the companies that clear and process trades for them, and the thirteen largest stock exchanges in the world. But it is only a dry run for a dry run; the industry plans a much bigger, more comprehensive test in the spring of 1999.

Of course, securities industry insiders note, all this testing is well and good, but the financial industry may still suffer if such things as electricity and phone service—which they cannot function without—are disrupted. This is why some participants said they were hoping their successful test would inspire some other industries, especially telecommunications, to follow suit.

Notes

1. February 17, 1998, Senate hearing at the State Capitol in Hartford, Connecticut.
2. Saul Hansell, "Georgia Bankers in Hot Millennium Water," *New York Times* (November 18, 1997). (See the online edition at www.nytimes.com.)
3. Andrew Cassel, "The First Victim of the 2000 Bug?" *Philadelphia Inquirer* (March 4, 1998).
4. "Securities Group: Year 2000 Tests OK," Associated Press (July 24, 1998).

CHAPTER 13

Will the Lights Stay On?

"We're no longer at the point of asking whether or not there will be any power disruptions, but we are now forced to ask how severe the disruptions are going to be."

—SENATOR CHRIS DODD, D-CONN., DURING A SENATE YEAR 2000 COMMITTEE INQUIRY INTO Y2K'S EFFECT ON ELECTRIC UTILITIES

Every now and then I meet someone who says something like, "I'm sure I'll be OK in the year 2000; my personal computer is only a year old." Or: "My personal computer is a Mac." I always have to refrain from asking, "But does your personal computer have a solar panel attached to it?"

One of the most troublesome aspects of the year 2000 problem is that it threatens a wide range of the very basic services that we take so completely for granted. It's difficult to give serious thought to the possibility of having to get along without them. Here's a brief look at how the glitch might affect some of these basic services.

Electricity

I mentioned in Chapter One that Gary North, one of the most negative Y2K prognosticators, believes it will cause a two-month failure of our electrical supply, which, he says, will be enough to end civilization as we know it. This is an interesting hypothesis—after all, very few of the institutions we count on could last that long on their backup supplies of power.

I do not believe, however, that the power interruption will be that dramatic or severe. Instead, many utility experts are predicting some sort of rolling brownout, from one part of the country to another, and lasting as long as a month or more. Unfortunately, there are so many different threats to electric utilities in this country (let alone in other countries) that it seems depressingly likely that Senator Dodd's assessment at the beginning of this chapter is accurate.

Remember that electric utilities are private companies, some large, some small, some with deep pockets and brand-new equipment, others less well-heeled and less modern. There are literally thousands of them across the country, and chances are that, like any other group of companies, they represent varying degrees of preparedness for the year 2000.

In Chapter One, I discussed how the year 2000 problem is often a matter of priorities. Thus, industries (and also geographic regions) that are in the midst of dramatic upheavals tend to be less prepared for Y2K because so much of their attention—especially the all-important attention of top management—has been focused elsewhere. Needless to say, this very thing is happening, big time, to electric utilities. At the very same time that they must cope with the year 2000 problem, they are also coping with deregulation, which for the first time ever allows electricity consumers to pick and choose among providers. It is the most fundamental change in this industry's history.

No wonder, then, that executives from the nation's top ten utilities didn't have all the answers at their fingertips when questioned by the Senate panel in June 1998. All of them said that their companies would be ready for the Y2K problems in time to prevent disruptions to service, but when faced with more detailed questions, their answers didn't inspire much confidence. Some did not even know the size of their companies' software portfolio. When asked how many of their essential computer systems had already been fixed, answers ranged from 54 percent to 5 percent to . . . not sure. Given the small amount of time left before the year 2000, and the number of different year 2000-related problems these companies must solve, none of this was encouraging. In most other industries, large companies have had much better, more organized Y2K projects than their smaller counterparts. If this tendency holds true in this industry, we can assume that the rest of the nation's more than eight thousand electric utilities are even less prepared than those that met with the panel.

Being distracted by deregulation is only part of the problem. Another is the industry's heavy dependence on embedded computer chips, which are often at the heart of the workings of a power plant. When these processors are confused, as they might be when they encounter the year "00," their most frequent response is to simply shut down, and take the entire plant with them.

How easily can this happen? Very easily. One engineer anonymously reported seeing a plant shut down each of three times that it was set to January 1, 2000. Disturbingly, the three shutdowns turned out to have been caused by three *different* chips.

Nuclear Plants (108 of Them)

Electric utilities differ profoundly from other types of companies in that they operate highly controversial, strictly regulated, and potentially deadly nuclear power plants, 108 of them in all, throughout the United States. The first, most obvious worry is that a year 2000 malfunction might cause a nuclear accident at one of these plants. Utility industry experts, however, agree that such a scenario is downright impossible.

But that doesn't mean that there's nothing to worry about. Less disturbing than the thought of a nuclear plant melting down—but still disturbing—is the thought of the plant shutting down and not being able to work at all. Nuclear plants are just as susceptible to date-sensitive logic chips as other electric plants are. But perhaps the greatest year 2000 danger they face is administrative: They may not be *allowed* to function.

Nuclear plants are overseen by the Nuclear Regulatory Commission, which, given the tremendous public distrust of nuclear plants, tends to follow a better-safe-than-sorry philosophy. The NRC is quite concerned about the year 2000 problem and, reasonably enough, is demanding assurances that the public has nothing to fear from a Y2K incident at a nuclear plant. In May 1998, it issued a letter to all plant license holders discussing the issue and demanding that they certify their plants in writing as year 2000-compliant by July 1999—or failing that, provide a status report and confirm that the plant would be ready by the year 2000.

From a year 2000 point of view, the demand is, if anything, mild. I for one would be nervous if the NRC asked for anything less. But will nuclear plants be able to meet this standard? At this writing, it's an open question, since most year 2000 studies show that utilities lag behind other types of industry in Y2K preparedness, and industry insiders say plant managers have been slow to appreciate the seriousness of the problem.

My guess is that most plant license holders will provide the asked-for certification, rather than risk being shut down. But what happens in July 1999 if the NRC finds a plant's status report and/or future work schedule inadequate? That plant may find itself forced to shut down no matter what assurances the license holder gives. If this happens on a wide scale, it'll be bad news for all of us, since some 20 percent of American electricity comes from nuclear plants, and in some regions (like the Northeast, where I live) the percentage is twice that.

There's yet another threat facing fuel-burning electricity plants, one that involves neither regulators nor logic chips: railroads. What do railroads have to do with electricity? Plenty. For reasons I'll explain later in this chapter, the year 2000 problem has a huge potential for interrupting shipping and transportation of all kinds. Most coal-powered electricity plants keep a few weeks' worth of coal on hand—enough to get them through any "normal" interruptions. But, Y2K is anything but a normal problem, and it may cause much-greater-than-normal interruptions. If this happens across the country, it may be difficult for many plants to get enough of the coal they need to keep running, or at least keep running at full capacity. Thus, as the actual year 2000 progresses, we may see a few waves of brownouts—not because the power plants aren't functioning properly, but simply because they have nothing to burn.

With all these different scenarios for the electricity supply to be interrupted by the year 2000 problem, it seems nothing more than mere caution for all of us to prepare for the possibility of a power interruption. Smart businesses should follow Prudential's example, preparing backup generators. They are a good idea in the home as well, and people (like me) whose houses are heated by devices controlled by electric switches—which usually shut down automatically in a power outage—should consider preparing alternative heat sources. In both cases, it's probably also wise to be prepared to relocate temporarily, though there's always the risk that the place you're planning to go to may have power problems of its own.

But all these preparations will only help if the outages are relatively short. Although it may not be true that two months without power would be enough to destroy Western civilization, it is true that there are limits to how well one can prepare for such an event. Generators, for instance, are great, but most of them are powered by gasoline, and gasoline pumps are powered by electricity. It's difficult to stockpile enough supplies to be meaningful during an extended outage—though a good supply of canned goods (and don't forget a hand-operated can opener) are probably a good idea.

Another good idea is to lay in an extra supply of bottled water. In many places, water is pumped and controlled by electricity, and if the lights go off, so do the taps. Furthermore, many water treatment and distribution plants are controlled by the same logic chips that might provoke a date-related failure in an electric plant. And private wells are almost always electric-powered.

Here again, however, it is only easy to prepare for a brief outage, especially for those businesses that depend on water as part of their manufacturing or other processes. It's difficult to imagine many Americans lugging buckets from the nearest natural body of water. On the other hand, this is a serious matter; no living thing can survive for long without a water supply.

Telephones ("Your Call Cannot Be Completed . . . .")

In my mind, one of the most frightening year 2000 prospects is that of picking up the phone and finding no dial tone. No way to call my mother in Florida. No way to conduct business, since most of the people I do business with are one hundred miles away or more. No way to read my e-mail—even though the Internet, which was designed to withstand a nuclear attack, stands a good chance of surviving the millennium rollover. No way to call the fire department if the house catches fire.

Telephone service is less crucial than electricity or water, but it's still pretty fundamental to most of our working and home lives. The Defense Department, television and radio transmissions, police and emergency personnel, banks, the Internet, and any number of other institutions are completely dependent on phone service, so much so that we usually take it for granted. This is why telecommunications along with banking and electrical power form the iron triangle of services whose serious disruption would likely threaten society as we know it.

How badly are phone systems threatened by the year 2000 problem? As with so many aspects of the glitch, the answer is not completely clear. I can't say with confidence, as I can of the banking industry, that the telecommunications industry is in pretty good shape, nor can I say with certainty that it isn't, as I can with electric utilities. What we have is a mixed bag, and what we may wind up with is a patchwork of working and nonworking systems, at least for a while.

To start with the good news, it is unquestionable that telecommunications as an industry began working on Y2K earlier than most others and is, generally speaking, ahead of the game. Several of the largest American phone systems have already banded together to conduct interconnectivity testing. In fact, at a July 31, 1998, Senate Committee hearing on telecommunications and the year 2000, Joseph Castellano, Bell Atlantic's network president, noted that "the level of confidence of major carriers is pretty high."

Are they too confident? Jim Woodward, senior vice president of Cap Gemini America, thinks they might be. "Telcos have a lot of technology they use to run their businesses and to provide services. It's quite varied and very high-tech," he says. In general, he believes, "telephone companies have started too late, are moving too slow, and are too optimistic about what they're accomplishing."

Which of these two views is right remains to be seen. What is clear now is that some segments of the telecommunications industry are worse off than others, and there are special reasons for concern.

The FCC Has No Teeth

Unlike the government agencies that oversee banking and power utilities, the Federal Communications Commission has few options if phone companies ignore year 2000 concerns. Some of them are doing just that. Recently, the FCC sent letters requesting information on year 2000 status to two hundred American telecommunications companies. Although large landline carriers responded quickly, and with the reassuring news that their Y2K projects were well under way, only eleven of the wireless companies contacted even bothered to answer the letters.

What can the FCC do about this? Not much. As a last resort, Senator Dodd has threatened that the Special Year 2000 Committee may release their names to the press.

The GPS Rollover

Months before the year 2000 itself arrives, many segments of the telecommunications industry (as well as banking, transportation, and many others) may be affected by an event that is completely unrelated and yet eerily similar to Y2K.

The Global Positioning Satellite System is a network of satellites, deployed by the U.S. Navy around the globe. Since GPS makes its signal freely available to anyone with a GPS receiver, and since it has one of the most accurate atomic clocks in the world, GPS has been used for years by all sorts of devices that need to synchronize with other devices—notably wireless transmission equipment, and also the network transmission equipment that handles most international calls.

Just as computers with two-digit fields are not technologically capable of counting past ninety-nine years, the GPS system for its own internal reasons is not technologically capable of counting past 1,023 weeks. It began counting weeks on January 6, 1980, and, by some odd coincidence, will reach 1,023 the week ending August 21, 1999. The week beginning August 22 will therefore be week zero, as far as the GPS is concerned. What happens then depends on how many of the millions of GPS receivers in use worldwide are ready for the change. But at the very least, it means that wireless communications companies are being hit by a double whammy: Y2K and the GPS rollover at the same time. The wireless industry's abysmal response to the FCC inquiry is a good clue that they may not be ready.

Small Phone Companies

There are more than one thousand small telephone companies in the United States, and, according to witnesses at the special committee hearing on telecommunications, they're moving a lot more slowly than their larger counterparts to respond to the year 2000 problem. (This means that the telecommunications industry is consistent with corporate America in general, where most large companies are very aware of the problem and doing something about it, while half of all small companies don't intend to do anything at all.)

Like other small companies, small telecommunications providers "may not realize or may be slow to realize the seriousness of the problem," according to FCC Commissioner Michael Powell. Even if they do recognize its urgency, Powell adds, they may not have the financial resources or personnel to do much about it.

Foreign Phone Companies

The United States is better prepared to deal with the year 2000 problem than any other nation on earth. This means that American companies and individuals who depend on overseas companies or governments have, to varying degrees, good cause to be concerned about how Y2K is likely to affect those relationships.

In no industry are companies as interdependent or—literally—interconnected as in telecommunications.

To make matters worse, telephone signaling carries date and time information embedded in it. This means that most phone companies are, to some extent, vulnerable to noncompliant signals from other companies, and there is serious concern as to whether most foreign phone companies, especially those in poorer countries, can correct the problem in time.

One big problem is "switch generics," the software that runs network exchanges, according to Frank Robert, managing partner with the Washington, D.C.-based consulting firm Comm-Strategies International and an affiliate of the Atlantic Advisory Group. Robert, who understands telecommunications in more detail than anyone I know, recently completed a Y2K project for a foreign telephone company with more than 10 million lines. He reports that worldwide providers of switch generics (such as Ericsson) are planning to offer compliant versions before the year 2000, but maybe not soon enough before calendar year 2000 for individual countries to reinsert the programming that makes these generics compatible with their particular phone systems.

"It's not right to assume that all developing countries will fail at this, of course," Robert adds. "But many will fail to meet the deadline in my opinion." He also says that "there are many kinds of network electronics beyond the main switch generics which will be affected. Network element managers that feed alarms to the control centers generally have time counters rather than conventional date representation, but many will be affected and not likely to be easily remediated by the conventional means [such as software tools that look for two-digit years]. Much outside-plant electronics is noncompliant, and many carriers don't even know how much of it they have and where it is."

There is, unfortunately, relatively little one can do to prepare for the absence of telephone service. If this comes to pass, it seems to me that many businesses have no choice but to close up shop until service is restored. Though Internet use is mostly dependent on phone service, communicating via e-mail can be an effective technique for getting messages through if phone service is sporadic. Voice mail can also be helpful in this respect.

Finally, an important concern for any business is to make sure its own PBXs or other in-house phone equipment will function properly in the year 2000. This is especially important for businesses (usually smaller ones) that have purchased the equipment used or from a third party and thus have had no direct contact with the manufacturer. In these cases, even a manufacturer that knows its equipment is noncompliant and wants to provide an upgrade has no way of knowing who you are or how to reach you. If this happens, no matter how well your phone service provider fixes its equipment it won't do you a whole lot of good.

You Can't Get There From Here

Although not part of the official iron triangle, there's another industry I believe is both threatened by the year 2000 problem and vital enough to bring some unraveling of modern society if it cannot function. I'm referring to transportation and shipping, the whole group of companies and industries that move people and products from point A to point B.

Make no mistake: We are a society that is tremendously dependent on these services, depending on trade among regions and with other nations to balance our need for products we can't produce or don't want to bother producing. Here is a simple and chilling example: About 95 percent of the components in the medicines we use are imported from other countries, and 70 percent of the world's supply of insulin comes from a single country, Denmark. What do we do if these products can't get here?

The Y2K threat to transportation is also the reason why some year 2000 pessimists are recommending stocking long-storage food, and why most of the millennial villages are located in agricultural regions. It's not so much that they fear a breakdown in farming, but a breakdown in the ability of farm products to reach the whole of the population—especially that part concentrated in urban areas.

Why is transportation a special concern? One obvious reason is that it is highly dependent on computers and computer chips, which manage travel and shipping schedules for millions of planes, ships, trains, and trucks and which also help operate many of the vehicles themselves. Another cause for concern is the double whammy I mentioned a little earlier, the rollover of the Global Positioning System. Telecommunications companies (and, incidentally, banks) depend on GPS for synchronizing timing devices. But, as its name suggests, GPS was primarily built to be a navigational tool. Countless organizations use it as exactly that; the GPS provides navigational information not only for the Defense Department's planes and guided missiles, but also for some ten million commercial planes and ships.

Ready for Takeoff?

Perhaps the mostly highly computer-dependent, and thus most vulnerable, area of the transportation industries is air travel. Airplanes operate by onboard computer chips, which may or may not be vulnerable to Y2K. So far, airplane manufacturers are quite optimistic. For instance, Tim Fehr, vice president of airplane systems at Boeing, recently told the Reuters news service that his staff conducted an exhaustive search for year 2000 flight safety risks in aircraft systems and found none.[1]

Fehr, along with Jane Garvey, head of the Federal Aviation Administration (FAA), is among the aviation officials who say they intend to be on board commercial airline flights as the clock strikes midnight on December 31, 1999. (In fact, Garvey, who's planning to fly from the East Coast to the West Coast, intends to fly through three different midnight hours across the continental United States!) All this is in response to popular concerns by ordinary citizens who fear that airplanes may fall cataclysmically from the sky.

Trust me, they won't. My concerns about air travel—and many other industries—are of a not-with-a-bang-but-a-whimper variety. That is, I think people are worrying about the wrong things. They focus on the threat of a meltdown at a year 2000-vulnerable nuclear power plant—an event that seems just about impossible—instead of worrying how their lives could be affected in very serious ways if the plants are perfectly safe but out of service. Likewise, I don't believe that a major airline or the FAA would be so foolish as to send a plane up into the sky without knowing that it could safely come down again. Especially given mounting worries about Y2K.

What does concern me, however, is this: There may be very real consequences if a significant number of flights can't get off the ground. Mail, package delivery, shipping of medicine, and any other transportation that is time-sensitive would be affected.

Is it really possible that planes might be grounded? Unfortunately, yes. My concern is not so much for the airlines, which are moving quickly to correct the problem. Airports are highly computer dependent too, and IATA, the International Air Transport Association (not to be confused with the ITAA, mentioned in earlier chapters), recently began comprehensive checks of major airports worldwide and is spending $19 million to create a comprehensive database of every major airport's compliance status.

The big problem here, it seems to me, is the FAA, which faces what seem impossibly daunting year 2000 challenges. Earlier this year, the agency received a round of criticism for its year 2000 planning, having announced plans to finish its year 2000 project in November 1999. That is cutting it close for any organization, but in the FAA's case the agency is managing its complex network of flight plans with forty mainframe computers built by IBM in the early 1970s. IBM has already stated that these mainframes will not work in the year 2000, which means the FAA will need to replace all forty of them.

Information technology professionals around the country scoffed at the thought of any organization undertaking such a massive project with only one extra month available to cover unforeseen delays. Add to this the fact that planes essentially never stop flying (cargo planes fly during the nighttime hours when there are fewer passenger flights). While it is fixing its year 2000 project, the FAA must also keep operating essentially twenty-four hours a day, 365 days a year.

"They won't be ready!" Peter de Jager flatly declared at a year 2000 conference in spring 1998.

But nobody likes bad publicity, least of all a government agency, and it wasn't long before the FAA declared that its year 2000 project would now be finished by June 1999. This represents a step in the right direction—if the agency really is able to keep to this schedule. The problem is that some observers suspect the agency may have "pencil-whipped" its problem. In other words, the original deadline seemed like a bad idea, so a new one was established without any regard to whether it was actually possible to meet it.

According to Joel Willemssen, director of civil agencies information systems at the General Accounting Office, it isn't possible. Willemssen told a House subcommittee in the summer of 1998 that his research showed the FAA was planning to pack an impossible amount of work into the months between now and June; for instance, its plans call for completing renovation on 42 of 157 systems in the same month.[2]

To make matters worse, FAA operations involve a tremendous amount of electronic data transfer, much of it with its counterparts in other countries. Here, again, there may be trouble: Willemssen said only 21 of the 90 nations to which U.S. airlines fly had supplied the FAA with any information at all on their year 2000 status.

Old Chips Slow Ships?

The picture doesn't look much brighter when it comes to surface transport, which, of course, handles the vast majority of the world's shipped goods. Much less information is widely available on these industries at this writing, in large part, I suspect, because they have not seriously begun addressing the issue yet. In March 1998, Ed Yourdon reported that he had just come from the maritime industry's first-ever year 2000 conference, where, he said, "people looked like they'd just been kicked in the stomach." Most were learning only for the first time the danger they were facing.

There are more than fifty computer chips on a typical modern ship, controlling everything from sprinklers and safety systems to communications to cargo loading equipment. Twenty to 30 percent of these chips may be date-sensitive, according to the International Group of Protection & Indemnity Clubs, which recently issued an official warning to ship owners about Y2K. Not only that, but port operations, cargo terminal systems, traffic management systems, and coast guard controls are all heavily computerized.

Railways face similar problems. When Union Pacific and Southern Pacific railroads merged in 1996, the resulting computer foul-up snarled trains across the western United States for months. It's not hard to imagine something similar happening if any of these systems isn't ready for Y2K. Then consider that traffic signaling systems are often controlled by outdated computer systems, and that even modern trucks and cars have embedded chips in them that could conceivably glitch, and the picture is complete.

What should you do? The multiple and very real threats to the entire transportation system worldwide are, I believe, the most powerful arguments for stockpiling anything and everything your company (or you) cannot function without. Even if your assessments show that your essential suppliers have their year 2000 problems well in hand, you could face crippling shortages if you or they depend on transport that turns out to be undependable.

Compounding the problem is the fact that if one transportation system fails, people and goods rush to use alternate systems, which usually overwhelms them. Anyone who had trouble sending a package by Federal Express during the UPS strike, or who's been caught in a traffic jam because a local commuter railroad wasn't operating normally, knows exactly what I'm talking about.

Notes

1. David Gersovitz, "Aviation World Moving Fast to Fix Millennium Bug," Reuters (June 9, 1998).
2. "Critics Charge FAA Missing Connections on Y2K Preparedness," *ITAA Year 2000 Outlook*, The Information Technology Association of America, Volume 3, No. 30 (August 7, 1998). (See www.itaa.org.)

CHAPTER 14

Ready to Spray?

Y2K Around the World

"It seems that the State Department had their Foreign Service Officers survey the governments where they were posted about the year 2000 problem. One officer, in an unnamed country, asked the local officials there how they intended to respond to the year 2000 millennium bug. He was told, 'Not to worry, my friend. We are prepared to spray anywhere and everywhere.' "

—REP. CONSTANCE A. MORELLA, DURING A HOUSE SUBCOMMITTEE ON TECHNOLOGY HEARING ON "THE GLOBAL DIMENSIONS OF THE MILLENNIUM BUG"

The United States can hardly claim to be completely ready for the year 2000 glitch. Gartner Group research shows most organizations have made too little progress in their year 2000 projects—if they have them at all. The General Accounting Office, among others, has warned repeatedly that most agencies of the federal government are so far behind in their Y2K fixes that many essential systems can't be repaired on schedule. Few organizations are able to fix every system in time.

None of this is very encouraging. Nevertheless, the United States is generally acknowledged to be readier for the year 2000 than any other nation on earth. According to the Gartner Group, the only other country that is anywhere near as far along in its year 2000 work is Australia. The rest are three months to two years behind.

It's an often-repeated truth that we now live in a global business community, where most companies are in some way affected by international commerce and where no country can hope to prosper for long if other regions are suffering hard times. As I write this in late summer 1998, that truth is being graphically illustrated by the financial markets. Although the U.S. economy is booming, a financial crisis in Russia has sent a wave of chaos through the world's financial markets, and the Dow Jones Industrial Average is down about 15 percent from its high earlier this year. What makes this even more surprising is that although Russia may be a military and technological powerhouse, economically speaking it's a weakling, with an economy about the same size as that of the Netherlands.

Given how much the nations of the world have to count on each other, the fact that the rest of the world is so ill-prepared for Y2K is bad news for all of us. But here are a few industries that may find themselves especially badly affected from an international perspective:

- *Telecommunications.* Telephone lines and satellites literally connect phones in every country on earth. In Chapter Thirteen, I described how phone companies in foreign countries, especially poorer countries, may have trouble getting their systems upgraded before New Year's Eve 1999. Some technology experts believe that if part of the international phone network goes down, it puts the entire system at risk.

- *Banking.* The banking and financial services industries are, of course, about as interconnected as our phone systems are. Further, these industries engage in massive amounts of electronic data interface (EDI), and most of their transaction messages contain dates. There are thus countless opportunities for banks to infect each other with the "millennium virus."

  In view of these dangers, there's been some talk of quarantining any bank that cannot show compliance. In the short run, this may be necessary to keep the world's banking system alive. In the long run, I believe, it would mean big trouble. First of all, it does not seem to me a viable way to manage financial transactions in our globally interconnected world. Worse, it creates a new category of global haves and have-nots.

- *Transportation.* Also in the last chapter, I discussed some of the threats to our national transportation network. Things look even grimmer when you consider international travel. Travel agencies, airports, ports, shipping authorities, customs authorities, air traffic control, and customs systems in other regions of the world mostly appear to be far behind the United States in year 2000 preparedness. Here again is an industry that largely depends on international agreements, conventions, and cooperation.

A Management Exercise?

One big problem is that many people in other countries do not appear to be taking the year 2000 problem seriously. At a recent Y2K conference, William Ulrich described a conversation with a business associate in Europe. It seems to this person that many European business executives believe they don't need to worry too much about Y2K because the whole thing was contrived by Americans as a management exercise.

Or there's the statement from Russia's Atomic Energy Ministry that I mentioned in Chapter Three: The Ministry plans to do nothing about Y2K since "we don't have any problems yet."

But even the growing number of international government and business leaders who do take Y2K seriously are often unable or unwilling to do much about it because they believe other problems have higher priority.

In some cases, it's hard to argue that they're wrong. If a nation's population can't buy enough food to survive, or is drinking poisoned water as a result of a flood, then even an interruption in power and phone service might seem minor if it's still months away. In other cases (introduction of the euro, for example), government leaders' priorities seem to be out of order. Either way, the result is the same: By the time this problem does achieve priority status, it will likely be too late to prevent serious disruptions.

Here's a look at how the year 2000 problem is being dealt with, or not being dealt with, in various regions of the world.

Canada, Australia, New Zealand, the United Kingdom, Israel

This may seem like an odd grouping of nations, but these are the countries besides the United States that are closest to being prepared for Y2K. In fact, a Merrill Lynch special report says that "the vast majority of replies to our Y2K Survey in Australasia—which are the islands of the South Pacific, including Australia, Tasmania, New Zealand, and New Guinea—seem almost too good to be true."[1] Gartner Group research shows Australia at roughly the same level of year 2000 readiness as the United States, and the rest of these countries are only three months or so behind.

Western Europe

Western Europe is one of the most highly computerized regions in the world, as computer dependent as anywhere. You'd think government leaders here would be very concerned about Y2K vulnerabilities, but they're not. In fact, they're so unconcerned that the government of the European Union has decided to launch the euro, its new international currency, in 1999. This is exactly the type of thing highly paid year 2000 consultants teach their corporate clients *not* to do: Introduce a major new technology project before year 2000 repairs are complete. The potential for the competing project to push the year 2000 project past its deadline is too great.

Here, we have a competing project not on a national but an international level, with eleven countries of the European Union scheduled to introduce the euro in the next year (Austria, Belgium, Finland, France, Germany, Ireland, Italy, Luxembourg, the Netherlands, Portugal, and Spain). Others are to follow by 2003.

Make no mistake, introducing the euro is a technology project of major proportions. Computers need to be reprogrammed to handle conversions from other currencies into and out of the euro (not to mention the extra keyboard keys and fonts needed to produce the new euro symbol). To make matters worse, as I noted in

Chapter 7, EU rules require "triangulation": All currency conversions in any country that uses the euro must be made through the euro.

Getting computers to do this is a massive reprogramming task. In fact, many experts believe the reprogramming required is actually a bigger project than year 2000 conversion. To make matters worse, the same programmers who are frantically working on Y2K, and being offered princely sums to use their outdated COBOL skills, are exactly the ones who are needed for euro conversion. No wonder Capers Jones calls the decision to introduce the euro now "one of the most unwise and hazardous public policy decisions in all of human history."[2]

Unfortunately, euro introduction affects not only the eleven countries involved but also all the countries that do business with them—which is to say, every country in the world. In fact, U.S. Federal Reserve chief Alan Greenspan has already complained that euro conversion work is interfering with Y2K efforts at his agency.

Not long ago, a year 2000 manager from an American computer company had a chance to talk with some European Parliament members who were in the United States to discuss the euro. She asked them how many year 2000 experts they'd consulted before determining their schedule for euro introduction. None, they admitted uncomfortably. But, they added, they were quite sure that launching the euro would not prevent the European community from solving its year 2000 problem in time. How did they know? Because that was one of the conditions for euro introduction.

That sounds reasonable, until you consider that the EU government has, in large part, staked its reputation on getting the euro out in time. A delay at this point would probably send shock waves through European, and then world, markets.

Besides, there's already plenty of evidence that euro conversion indeed impedes year 2000 remediation. Jones predicts that more than 35 percent of mission-critical repairs won't be done in Western Europe because of euro conversion. The Gartner Group claims that most of Western Europe is already nine months behind the United States in year 2000 work. How much more is needed before the Europeans acknowledge that there is a conflict?

Asia

Government and business leaders in Asia are also likely to be too distracted to deal with Y2K. In this case the reason is not public policy decisions but an economic crisis that has, as I write this, been gripping the region for nearly a year. As economist Ed Yardeni notes in his **Netbook** (see www.yardeni.com), "Many companies and financial institutions in Asia have a year 1998 problem, namely, staving off bankruptcy. Y2K is likely to remain a low priority for managers and funding until it is too late."

Though the Gartner Group puts Japan ahead of the rest of the region in its Y2K readiness, local observers report a shocking lack of urgency over the issue. They point out that much of Asian banking is dependent on IBM software written in the 1970s and by now customized beyond recognition. IBM no longer supports the software, and much of it has to be reprogrammed to achieve year 2000 compliance. A further problem is that much of Japanese industry relies on just-in-time inventory, which increases year 2000 vulnerability. (I discuss just-in-time dangers in more detail in Chapter Eight.)

Year 2000 watchers in other Asian countries mostly report that the situation is even worse. One exception is Taiwan, where the government has promised to shut down banks, nuclear plants, and airlines that can't pass a year 2000 inspection by mid-1999. Without going into too much more country-by-country detail, the bottom line is this:

1. Many Asian countries are highly computerized and very dependent on information systems and software. Some of these systems are clearly old enough to present serious year 2000 risks.

2. The ongoing economic crisis (along with other major changes, such as Japan's "big bang" financial deregulation) is likely to distract many Asian decision makers well into 1999, by which time it is probably too late to stave off some year 2000 disruptions.

3. Unlike American companies, which (if publicly traded) must face up to the Securities and Exchange Commis-

sion, most Asian companies do not at this time have to report their year 2000 status to any government agency. Furthermore, it is consistent with most Asian cultures to keep one's troubles private. It is therefore difficult for outsiders to properly assess risk levels at many Asian businesses, large and small, at least until things start to go seriously wrong, at which point it will be too late.

Russia

This is another country where economic troubles have completely overwhelmed year 2000 concerns. I noted earlier in this chapter that Russia's current economic woes have brought down financial markets from Wall Street to Tokyo. The ruble is in free fall, turning Russian bank accounts to dust. President Boris Yeltsin, who has for years held the country together by force of personality, seems ill and distracted on the rare occasions when he appears in public at all. Communists are threatening to turn back the clock on free-market reforms, while Russia's Western trading partners fret over their investments.

In short, it seems highly unlikely that Y2K is the chief worry on anybody's mind.

Indeed, taken in the context of what must seem like a nonstop state of emergency, the Russian Atomic Energy Ministry's let's-wait-and-see-what-happens attitude seems a lot less outlandish. The problem is that Russia is still a fairly computer-dependent state whose infrastructure is strained under the best of circumstances, and whatever its other problems, the country cannot afford to simply ignore the year 2000 problem.

An unfortunate bit of timing is that the country's next presidential election is scheduled for 2000, and Yeltsin has promised not to run again. Of course, this is the sort of political promise that should never be taken as gospel, but if the president is indeed suffering from ill health, he may not be able to continue in office. Given all this, it seems highly likely that there will be a hotly contested political struggle taking shape at exactly the same time that the nation is finally forced to deal with its year 2000 problem.

The Developing World

I've lumped quite a number of countries into this category, which covers some of Southeast Asia, Eastern Europe, Latin America, and Africa. These are widely divergent countries, with varied year 2000 problems, of course, but many of them face a similar Y2K outlook. It can be summed up as follows:

1. Awareness of year 2000 issues is generally low. In fact, very few developing countries have even set up a national office to address the problem.

2. Funds for year 2000 remediation (as for many other projects) are extremely limited.

3. In general, these are not highly computer-dependent societies, which, locals and leaders are hoping, lessens the impact of the Y2K bug.

4. On the other hand, many developing nations face huge infrastructure problems. Telecommunications systems and power systems that are already stretched to the limit may unravel badly if they aren't year 2000-compliant. This is why year 2000 discussions with representatives of developing nations often focus on matters of embedded chips and infrastructure. Furthermore, wherever developing nations are vulnerable to Y2K, they're very vulnerable, since they're likelier than richer countries to be working with older, noncompliant hardware and software.

Some help is on the way from the World Bank, which last year recognized the special risks developing nations were facing. The bank's infoDev project, which focuses on technology in developing countries, has started a special year 2000 project with funding from the United Kingdom, and, more recently, the United States. The project provides both conferences and teleconferences for government and business leaders, networks where they can exchange information, and grants of up to $500,000 to get national Y2K projects started. (The bank may also offer loans in the more substantial sums that doubtless are needed to complete these projects.)

Y2K Brings Some Benefits

In addition to all its dangers, the year 2000 problem has proved to be something of an opportunity for certain developing nations, especially India and some countries of Eastern Europe, where education levels are often higher than employment opportunities, and knowledge of English is widespread. Many Western countries have taken advantage of local unemployment and low wages by either bringing in programmers from these countries, or, more commonly, shipping their year 2000 reprogramming and testing work via the Internet to software "factories" where local programmers do the work. Some of these vendors now also believe they will see similar benefits from euro conversion work, keeping local programmers busy for years to come.

All this software work is providing a major boost for these developing economies, just when they need it most. But the benefits of the glitch probably aren't enough to offset the harm it will do if developing nations turn out to have severe infrastructure disruptions. There's a further danger, that with all the local programming talent working on Y2K projects from abroad, these nations' own year 2000 repairs may not be finished in time.

Notes

1. Merrill Lynch, "Y2K: Implications for Investors" (June 1998).
2. Capers Jones, *The Year 2000 Software Problem: Quantifying the Costs and Assessing the Consequences* (Addison Wesley, 1997).

CHAPTER 15

What If . . . ?

Contingency Planning

"I'll tell you a story I heard from a computer scientist who's been involved with the Department of Defense. There is a nuclear waste site in southern Washington State. It runs along the Columbia River, in a very beautiful area.

"The nuclear waste site is run by a computer system. It's an old computer system and will not function properly when the year rolls over to 00. The people went in to take a look at that system to see what it would take to fix it, determined that fixing it was not an option, for whatever reason—the language used, or a problem with shutting it down—and couldn't figure out what to do about it.

"So they're building another containment system around the existing containment system, to be run by another computer that will be year 2000-compliant. That is a contingency plan."

—William Ulrich

If you've read this far, then you know that the year 2000 problem has the potential to disrupt your business—and your home life—in a huge variety of ways. Ultimately, there are only two types of things that you can do to prepare:

1. Do what you can to correct or replace non-year 2000-compliant hardware, software, and suppliers, avoiding year 2000 malfunctions before they happen.
2. Plan ahead, so that you'll know exactly what to do in the very likely event that you encounter some year 2000 disruptions.

No matter how successful you are—or think you are—at preventing year 2000 mishaps, you really need to do both of these things, because if systems fail—and especially if they fail in unexpected ways—good contingency planning can easily make the difference between staying in business and going belly-up. The very nature of Y2K is that things do fail in unexpected ways.

I really would like to explain what to do to absolutely guarantee that you and your business will not suffer because of any year 2000 disruption. Unfortunately, I can't. There aren't any such guarantees—unless, perhaps, you're willing to move to one of the new millennial villages and join in learning nineteenth-century farming techniques (see Chapter Three).

Dealing with Y2K means assessing risk, and mitigating that risk as much as is reasonably possible. The key word in the previous sentence is "reasonably," because if everything that can conceivably go wrong does go wrong, then the people who've been predicting that Y2K means the end of Western civilization may prove to be right. There aren't many practical steps you can take to prepare for something like that.

But if there are only small-to-moderate disruptions in such things as the supply chain and electrical power, if the year 2000 problem causes a host of malfunctions, without creating complete chaos—my best guess as to what will happen—then there are things you can do to prepare, if not for the worst, then for the relatively bad.

The basic idea is to look at every function in your organization that is vulnerable to the year 2000 problem and ask yourself what you will do if the function is interrupted. In many cases, the answers are decidedly unappealing, and these may be steps that you hope not to have to take. Nevertheless, you are better off planning for them.

Here are some questions you should ask yourself, and some possible answers to consider.

What If Our Computers Stop Working?

This is the most basic level of contingency planning, the part that's most under your control, and thus the part you should probably do first. This is also where you have the most options. Here are a few.

System Contingency

Backing up a computer system with another computer system may sound futile, but in a lot of cases this may be a step worth considering. In an organization that has both a mainframe and a small inventory of desktop PCs, it might make sense to have software on hand that can reproduce some of the most essential functions from the mainframe on some of the desktops.

System contingency only makes sense, of course, if the backup system has been rigorously tested for year 2000 compliance and the setup includes a bridge or other system that prevents the noncompliant system from contaminating the compliant one with two-digit years. Of course, if the two systems perform identical functions, with the only difference being that one is compliant, it makes more sense to simply switch to the new system in the first place.

Do It by Hand

Many, perhaps most, computer functions can be done manually, and for countless organizations this is the bottom-line contingency: If our computers aren't working, we'll just do it by hand.

Fine, in theory. In practice, it won't be easy. A year 2000 consultant I once met described what she called a typical conversation on this issue with a typical corporate department head:

> *Department head:* It's not a problem. We did it manually for years. We'll just go back to the way we used to do things before these stupid computers came along.
>
> *Y2K consultant:* OK. How much business was your department responsible for in those days?
>
> *Department head:* Oh, about $4 million a year.
>
> *Y2K consultant:* How much are you responsible for now?
>
> *Department head:* About $10 million.

Y2K consultant: I see. How many people did you have in your department then?

Department head: Around forty.

Y2K consultant: Uh-huh. And how many do you have now?

Department head: Ten.

Y2K consultant: And do any of these ten people remember how to do it manually?

Department head: Well, Myrtle does, but I think she's retiring next month . . .

I could go on, but you get the idea. There's a reason computers have been adopted nearly universally by businesses all over the world: They are enormously more efficient at many tasks than human beings are. Remove the computer, and you lose all that efficiency. It is therefore impossible for a company to replace all or even most of its computer functions with manual functions, unless it is willing to dramatically expand its workforce. (This is why Bill Ulrich recommends temporary clerical services as a good investment for the year 2000.)

Nevertheless, doing it manually is the only possible contingency for some tasks, and in those cases you have no choice but to make that your contingency plan. If you do, I recommend the following:

1 Make sure that at least some of the people who need to do the manual job know how to do it before a year 2000 problem strikes. (If, say, the department manager is well versed in manual methods, he or she can teach the rest of the department what to do, should the need arise.)

2 Make sure that any paper forms (billing and the like) that might be needed for this manual task are in stock and available.

3 Plan for manual replacement on an absolute minimum number of tasks. Otherwise, if several year 2000 malfunctions strike at once, the people doing these jobs quickly find themselves overloaded.

Get Someone Else to Do It

Some of the tasks you depend on your computer systems to do can probably be outsourced to another company. This may not be an ideal solution, but as we have seen, if you do have year 2000 malfunctions in mission-critical systems, you will probably not be able to replace them all inhouse.

Since we're talking contingency planning, it probably makes sense to do an evaluation now of essential jobs that an outside firm can do, and then negotiate those relationships, before the year 2000 arrives and competition for such services mounts. Set in place whatever arrangements you require to guarantee that they are available, if needed.

But before you put this contingency in place, make absolutely sure that (1) the company you're sending work to has its own year 2000 problem under control well enough that its ability to deliver your work on schedule is not compromised, and (2) whatever delivery systems you need (phone lines for data, shipping, etc.) also have backups and alternatives available in case of year 2000 disruptions. After all, it does you little good to outsource, say, forms processing if the processed forms remain trapped at their location because the delivery service that should have brought them isn't working.

Live Without It

I said these aren't all going to be attractive options, and I meant it. By now, you may be sick of the word *triage*, but in its original, wartime use, it referred to a method that kept the maximum possible number of soldiers alive. Life and death can be a useful way of looking at the question of how you choose which functions really *have to* get done.

Will you be forced to close your doors tomorrow, if you can't do this task? Next week? Next month? At the very least, you should prepare to choose among mission-critical functions, and also to deal as best you can with whatever consequences arise from not being able to do everything that you normally consider essential.

What If Our Devices That Contain Embedded Chips Stop Working?

It depends, first of all, on what these devices are doing. If yours is a manufacturing operation and you have embedded chips in robotics or other automatic devices that help make whatever it is you make, then your choices are pretty much the same as those mentioned above: Replace the devices with others that don't have date-sensitive chips, do the work manually, outsource it, or get along without it.

For other types of devices, backups may be readily available. For example, if your copiers and fax machines are affected, a local copying center may be able to help. Many types of equipment can be rented or used at alternate offsite locations.

A very big problem arises if embedded chips or other system problems trip up your company's telecommunications equipment. Functioning phones are mission-critical to just about every business, so this is a contingency that requires careful forethought. Options might include having mobile phones on hand, a few old-fashioned single-line phones available to partially replace nonworking systems, and using a local phone company's voice-mail service.

As always, whatever backup systems you prepare, make very sure they themselves will not be rendered inoperable by Y2K. Ideally, they should either be guaranteed Y2K-compliant by their manufacturers or completely analog (as in the case of a rotary phone).

What If Our Suppliers Are Affected by Year 2000 Malfunctions?

In Chapter Eight, I discussed in some detail how to assess year 2000 risk at your essential suppliers, and how to prepare in case they can't deliver as planned. I mention it again here because preparing backup suppliers for any materials or services your organization can't get along without is an essential part of contingency planning. You may wind up stockpiling, or having them inventory extra supplies (but keep the possibility of transport interruptions in mind if you choose this option), or preparing contingency relationships with other suppliers. As always, the important thing is to plan ahead.

What If Our Customers Are Affected by Year 2000 Malfunctions?

This is a possibility I haven't discussed so far, but it poses as great a risk as that of a year 2000 problem with an essential supplier. If a significant number of customers—or a single significant customer—is temporarily or permanently disabled by Y2K, your company could unexpectedly lose needed revenues. This could also happen if the customer continues functioning normally but is no longer able to pay you in a timely manner.

What should you do? Needless to say, lining up replacement customers may be more difficult than lining up replacement suppliers, but you are one step ahead if you make plans to do this ahead of time. This is also one of many good reasons why smart organizations keep lots of cash available as the year 2000 approaches, so as to make up for unexpected shortfalls.

You can minimize the likelihood of facing this particular problem by paying attention now to your customers' year 2000 readiness. This might mean handing out flyers, passing on information, or even, if appropriate, offering to do a year 2000 assessment for them.

What If Elements of Our Local Infrastructure Fail?

Find and plan for your least unattractive option in any of these cases:

1. *Power outage.* This is the possibility that has led Prudential to have generators on site at some of its locations. Having generators on hand, or at least available, is probably a good idea, although generators can only provide power in the short term. In the (hopefully unlikely) event of a prolonged outage, you will probably be forced to either close your doors for a while, or temporarily relocate, if power is available elsewhere.

2. *Water interruption.* Here again, if there is more than a very short-lived problem, you'll probably have to close or go elsewhere.

3 *Facilities problems.* If your building's elevators aren't working, you might encourage your staff to climb the stairs to work. (Keep in mind that disabled, pregnant, or elderly staff members might not be able to do this.) Another option might be to temporarily relocate to a lower floor. Since the year 2000 problem will strike in January, though, you probably can't stay in your offices if there is no heat (unless, of course, you're located in the Sun Belt).

4 *Telephone outage.* First, make sure that the problem lies with your local phone company, not your in-house equipment. Here again, mobile phones might be useful. It also might help to plan tasks that employees can work on for a while without using the phone, such as working with old files.

5 *Transportation shutdown.* Consider making car pool plans, or planning for telecommuting, in case staff members suddenly find they can't take public transportation to work. You may also have a big problem if the service or services you count on to send your products to customers (or bring in essential supplies) cannot function normally. Experiences such as the 1997 UPS strike have shown that when one service stops working, the others are immediately overloaded. So now is probably a very good time to ask yourself who else could do your shipping for you.

Contingency Planning at Home

Contingency planning should go beyond the workplace. Here are some relatively simple steps you should take at home, to make sure your everyday life is disrupted by the year 2000 glitch as little as possible.

1 *Prepare for power outages.* Actually, I believe everyone everywhere should be prepared to do without electric-

ity for a couple of days, since even major cities experience blackouts once in a while. This means stocking flashlights (along with a few sets of fresh batteries!), candles, or, better yet, oil lamps and lamp oil. Most homes also depend on electricity for water, and though their heating systems may not be electric-powered, they are often controlled by electricity and do not work if the power is off. Therefore, you should also consider stocking a few gallons of bottled water, and (assuming there is winter where you live) extra blankets. Depending on what type of home you have, an alternate heat source such as a kerosene lamp or wood stove might also be a good idea.

Another alternative might be to purchase a generator, but if you decide to do this then the sooner you do it, the better. Demand already seems to be rising.

2 *Prepare alternative transportation methods.* In the unlikely event that your car contains a date-sensitive computer chip, or public transportation isn't working, you should know what alternatives (taxi services, buses, etc.) are available.

3 *Stockpile long-storage food.* I don't agree with predictions of food riots, and I sincerely believe there won't be severe food shortages. However, I must acknowledge that there are about a dozen different ways that the year 2000 problem could make it difficult to get your regular shopping done. Having some extra canned goods, dried foods, and other long-storage items squirreled away seems like simple common sense.

4 *Stockpile medicines.* Especially if there are any medicines you really need. This is a very important measure, since the pharmaceutical industry is dependent on importing, which may very well be affected by Y2K.

5 *Have extra cash on hand.* The second half of 1999 is probably not the ideal time to make a big-ticket purchase or

> do anything else that stretches your finances to the limit. The possibility that some aspect of the year 2000 could require extra money, either to tide you over if your salary is interrupted or otherwise compensate for some problem, just seems like too big a concern to ignore.

But I'd also recommend having some cash around in the most literal sense: extra currency in case of any short-term problems at the bank—or getting to the bank—in the early days of the year 2000. Enough to get you through a couple of weeks is probably a good idea.

If you're the year 2000 trailblazer for your organization, you can do your coworkers a big favor by passing this advice on to them. Even those year 2000 skeptics who scoffed at the problem a year ago are probably grateful now for any suggestions, as general Y2K fears widen. This helps your organization as well. After all, people who feel safe from year 2000 concerns in their homes are probably more effective in the workplace.

CHAPTER 16

After the Time Bomb

Surviving in the Post-2000 World

"There is only one computer that is guaranteed to work on January 1, 2000 and it will give you all the information you need. Every one of you has one, sitting on top of your shoulders. All your employees have one, too, and you don't need to upgrade the BIOS. And it will work.

"But you need to remember to use it."

—Leslie Schelp, head of the year 2000 program at Tandem Computers

According to legend, an astronomy professor was once asked to write a five-hundred-word article on whether there might be life on Mars. He wrote "Nobody knows" 250 times.

Forbes magazine referred to this story in discussing year 2000 prognostications.[1] The magazine has a point: It's pretty much impossible for anyone—even those of us who've studied the question in depth—to predict with precision or certainty what the world will look like after New Year's Day 2000. I do believe that it will be easier to tell by the time this book appears than it is as I write it. Here's a simple test: What happened in the first few months of 1999?

Why should this be an effective test? In Chapter Two, I discuss how Y2K isn't waiting for calendar year 2000, and that many programs begin including the year 00 in their calculations starting in 1999. This means that 1999 is something of a smaller-scale dry run for the real century rollover.

Beyond question, there will be computer malfunctions. They're already happening. But these are not obvious to most people because so far they have been limited enough to be contained, and none has amounted to a real disaster.

Is this still the case in early 1999? If so, there's a good chance we may all get through January 1, 2000, without the kind of mishaps that will probably be seen in Warner Brothers' planned disaster movie *Y2K*. But if not, if there are lots of problems and mistakes and screw-ups, then expect the year 2000 to be much, much worse.

Even before 1999, it's possible to make some educated guesses that you can use for planning purposes. Keeping in mind that these are just that, educated guesses and not absolute certainties, here are some changes you might expect for the first few years of the next millennium.

There Will Be Some Level of Disruption

There are two reasons that absolute year 2000 predictions are difficult. The first is that these disruptions tend to be completely unpredictable; in most cases it's hard to know whether or how something is going to break unless you're already fixing it. The second reason is that people's responses are themselves difficult to predict. Year 2000 prognosticators who believe there will be a complete breakdown of systems and services are assuming that most businesses and governments can do little or nothing to fix the year 2000 problem.

Undeniably, Y2K has been ignored for too long, and even now it is not receiving the attention it needs in many organizations. But it's wrong to assume that nobody is doing anything effective about it. What I believe will happen is something midway between the no-big-deal year 2000 that skeptics are planning for and the complete chaos that Gary North and other doomsayers are expecting.

I expect some failures, but not a complete breakdown, in electricity and transportation, and possibly in some aspects of telephone service. Banking should proceed with few interruptions. Government services will probably be affected, but I believe the most essential ones will manage to keep going.

This is why, in Chapter One, I stressed flexibility as one of the best responses to possible year 2000 malfunctions. It may be difficult to predict exactly what shape these take and where (or even when) they may strike, but the likelihood of some disruption is too great to ignore.

Globalization Will Be Put to the Test

Study after study has alerted the year 2000 community to the fact that the nations of the world are facing the year 2000 problem with different levels of preparedness; the United States is at the head of the pack. Lagging farthest behind are the poorer nations of Eastern Europe, Africa, Southeast Asia, and Latin America—countries that have only in recent years begun joining the world business community meaningfully.

As I write this, deepening economic crises in Russia and Asia have dampened the West's enthusiasm for pouring money into these regions—and this is before most Western investors have taken Y2K into consideration. When they do, things are likely to get worse. A year 2000 consultant confided recently that one of his clients was simply "writing off" its properties in developing countries that are clearly not ready to deal with the glitch in time.

Some business and government leaders in developing countries are counting on their lesser dependency on technology to protect them from Y2K. Indeed, it's often noted that half the world's population has never used a telephone, and one could easily assume that people who are so untouched by technology are unlikely to care, or even notice, if the year 2000 problem affects computers and computerized devices.

But is this a valid assumption? Given the interconnected nature of today's world, I'm not so sure. I would argue that even a village family, living without electricity or phone service, might feel the secondhand effect of a systemic breakdown in, say, the level of health care they receive or the prices they get for the products they bring to the local market. Either way, it seems pretty clear that developing nations are very vulnerable to the year 2000 problem, more so than their leaders may have initially thought. The World Bank's year 2000 program described in the last chapter is a commendable effort, but it is almost certainly too little, too late.

What happens when the developing world gets hit by the millennium bug? The banking industry has already discussed shutting out banks that are not year 2000-compliant from international electronic networks, and it's easy to imagine something similar happening—perhaps even unintentionally—with international phone networks. It may be very tempting for Western partners to simply write off their third-world contacts, as the company that I mentioned is planning to do. Especially if they're struggling to deal with year 2000 disruptions of their own.

Y2K Will Affect the World Economy

In fact, I believe it already has. I'm writing this chapter in September 1998, as the New York Stock Exchange faces its worst decline in a decade, having in a couple of weeks undone all the gains of the past year. Beyond any doubt, the slide was triggered by the economic crisis in Russia and continuing doldrums in Asia.

But there are two other factors closer to home that are probably having an impact on the market: Some companies have seen disappointing earnings in the second half of this year, and, more significantly, American productivity has ceased growing in the last couple of months, for the first time in several years.

There are many reasons for companies to see lower earnings, but for some companies the tens and even hundreds of millions they're spending on year 2000 remediation is certainly part of the equation. The connection is clearer when you consider the slowdown in productivity growth. Beyond question, much of the last decade's productivity gains have come from technological innovations. Now, much of the brainpower that went into building newer and better technology is focused instead on keeping existing technology working when the millennium bug hits.

How deep will the impact be? It's hard to say, but Ed Yardeni's prediction of a recession comparable to 1973–1974 certainly seems reasonable. Inevitably, world stock markets will suffer as, increasingly, laypeople begin panicking over Y2K.

But however bad the effect is, I do not believe it will be very long lasting. The worst of the year 2000 disruptions should be over, and the bulk of remediation done, by 2002 or 2003. Once it is all safely behind us, both our information technology industry and our businesses themselves will be better off than they were before (read on, for more about this). This is not to say, of course, that the world economy will necessarily be booming; other non-Y2K factors could also take their toll.

Technology Changes Forever

The year 2000 problem may have only a temporary effect on the world's economy, but its effect on the information technology industry is profound and permanent. Dealing with Y2K forever changes both the information technology field itself and how technology interacts with other business functions.

For a look into the future of software development I called Ian Hayes. Here are some of his thoughts on what the future of technology might look like.

There Will Be an Antitechnology Backlash

"We're about to validate the view of the world's Ted Kaczynskis [the technology-hating Unabomber]," Hayes notes. So far, I haven't seen any of this antitechnology sentiment, but then, there haven't been any large and public Y2K snafus yet either.

As I explained in Chapter Three, I believe that, on the contrary, the year 2000 problem proves that we've come to expect technology to be absolutely reliable, so much so that airplanes, life-support machines, and nuclear devices are all routinely controlled by computer, and most of us don't give this matter a second thought.

I don't, however, expect most people to agree with this logic. So many people already seem to view computers as unreliable and supremely suspicious that Hayes may well be correct.

He further predicts that as technology gets a black eye, young people choosing careers will tend to opt for other disciplines with better reputations. Given that the year 2000 problem has driven programmer salaries into the stratosphere, I'm not sure I agree that prospective programmers will be so eager to turn to other careers. But if he's right and I'm wrong, then expect the current shortage of qualified technology folks to get even worse, and the market for hiring expert technology help even tighter. ITAA says its research shows the programmer shortage is already enough to undercut many companies' growth; expect this problem to get worse.

Expect More Software Litigation—Lots More

"Software litigation is going to be the ambulance chasing of the future," Hayes predicts.

His logic is simple, and compelling. Two factors, he says, have historically prevented lawyers from aggressively pursuing software-based lawsuits. The first was the difficulty of explaining complex computer technology questions to a jury. The second was the lack of past legal precedents, to establish acceptable standards of care.

But as I noted earlier, many lawyers, and even whole law firms, have enthusiastically jumped into the year 2000 fray, and they will emerge having learned how to explain software to laypeople. Likewise, the cases that are decided over year 2000 issues will create the precedents lawyers have been waiting for. As Hayes says, it is unlikely that they will all go back to whatever they were doing before.

Software Developers Will Be More Accountable

Nobody likes the idea of medical malpractice suits, but, Hayes points out, lawsuits instilled standards and codes into the medical profession that have probably saved lives. Likewise, with the possibility of software litigation looming, software developers need to take more responsibility for what they produce.

This is probably not a bad thing. When Hayes gives presentations on the software industry after 2000, he uses a toaster nestled in its original packaging to illustrate how unfair the software industry is to most users. If the toaster were software, he notes, the user would, by opening the package, agree to a host of restrictions on toaster use that are packed inside. Meanwhile, the toaster company would offer no guarantees that the toaster would even approximate its stated purpose.

Anyone who's bought shrink-wrapped software recently should have a pretty good idea what he's talking about. The reason computer purchasers have so far had no choice but to accept these egregious contracts is that no one has legally challenged them.

I add to this prediction my own view that future legislation is likely to put responsibility for software on developers' shoulders. The reason is that there is a battle shaping up in Congress between the business community, which wants to limit its liability for year 2000 glitches, and the legal community, which emphatically does not want limits on possible Y2K lawsuits. Blaming the people and organizations who created the software in the first place may be the one idea on which the two groups can agree.

With liabilities attached, programming will have to evolve from the freewheeling profession it is now to something with many more standards and practices, something more akin to engineering, Hayes believes. No one will regret the passing of the days of wild-eyed, sleepless, pizza-munching programmers more than I, but in the long run I think that if programmers become serious professionals, it will be good for both their profession and the organizations they serve.

If nothing else, the need for year 2000 remediation has revealed a host of problems such as lost code, poor documentation, and such things as naming date fields after programmers' family members and pets (see Chapter Two). The sometimes-intentional result is to make it nearly impossible for any subsequent programmers to alter, or even understand, the software in question. Changing these practices alone is a step in the right direction.

The Role of Technology Will Change Within Businesses

In Chapter Two, I described what seems to be a disturbing lack of understanding, or even friendliness, between many corporate managers and their technology staff. Hostilities seem to exist on both sides. Some technology people, aware that there is no such thing as corporate loyalty anymore, have seemed willing to use their jobs as a chance to work with new technology and gain greater technical knowledge, even if it means ignoring the year 2000 problem and thus putting the whole organization at risk. Business leaders (many of whom are from a generation that tends to mistrust computers) seem to think of technology as necessary evil at best. Hayes reports that many executives use the term "black hole" when describing their information systems departments: You keep pouring in money and manpower, and only occasionally does anything positive result.

Dealing with Y2K only serves to make this situation worse. Some business executives are already quite angry at the prospect of spending a substantial portion of their budget to fix systems that were supposed to be working just fine. As Hayes points out, focusing on "core competencies" is a popular management idea these days—and top managers faced with spending big bucks to fix programs with two-digit dates may conclude that software is not among their organizations' core competencies.

To make matters worse, most companies of any size have had to bring in outside vendors to deal with the year 2000 problem. As a result, management may decide that outsourcing is a better idea and reduce the information technology department, or eliminate it altogether.

Every Glitch Has a Silver Lining

Believe it or not, there are some positive aspects to dealing with the year 2000 problem, and some ways in which dealing with it does our organizations and our society lasting good. I don't mean to suggest for a moment that the good points outweigh the bad. But, since we're stuck with it anyway, consider the following.

Competitive Advantage

Companies that have acted swiftly, decisively, and preferably early to combat the millennium bug have a definite advantage if their competitors find themselves unable to operate as usual because of year 2000 malfunctions.

But you don't even have to wait until something goes wrong. As concern over Y2K grows, both in the business community and among the public at large, any organization that can show it's got the problem under control should reap benefits in the form of customer confidence and industry stature. Indeed, those businesses that have had well-organized year 2000 projects for the past two or three years are seeing those rewards right now.

Better Inventory of Software and Hardware

I mentioned in Chapter Four economist Paul Strassman's argument that what created Y2K in the first place was the attitude that software is an expense rather than an asset. In fact, it is an asset, and one result of even a limited year 2000 project is that the value of the asset is much improved.

Besides being year 2000-compliant, the remediated software is likely to be more dependable too, for one simple reason: It has been tested. Hayes points out that most companies have never adequately tested their software. Often, they simply relied on end users to find and report problems. Many of them are now learning how to test software for the first time. Further, a company that's been burned by, say, missing source code (see Chapter Two) is unlikely to let the code go astray again.

In addition to improving the software itself, conducting a year 2000 program brings a second benefit. For the first time, many companies know exactly what hardware and software they have, and exactly where it is within the organization. All in all, dealing with Y2K means a substantial improvement in software portfolios worldwide, and in the long run this is a fundamental advantage.

Better Understanding of Our Essential Business Functions

In a recent article, Peter de Jager argues that most of our technology is "bloated with things we want, not things we need."[2]

As an example, he says, an inventory system really needs to do four things and four things only: add stock, pull it, query for availability, and allow corrections. "This is not acceptable today," he points out. "It is only acceptable when the real system fails and you tell management it'll take three months to fix. Then they'll sit you down, and explain to you, in clear, concise language, what's necessary to run the business. You'll deliver what they need in three days."

I'm not sure all problems can be solved quite so quickly, but I think de Jager has a very good point about technological bloat. It seems to me the information technology industry has spent the last twenty years in a mad race to add functionality of every possible kind to every possible system. (As I write this, I'm listening in the background to a C/Net report about a microwave oven/computer that has a touch-sensitive screen and voice recognition and helps you do your banking while you're cooking dinner. . . .) If dealing with Y2K forces us to winnow our technology down to what's really necessary, useful, or important, that might be a very good thing.

It is an even better thing if going through this process forces us to do the same with what we do every day. Preparing for the year 2000 offers an opportunity (admittedly unwelcome) to figure out exactly what the tasks are that really need to get done for our businesses, and perhaps our lives as well.

The year 2000 problem is here. We can't wish it away, we can't ignore it, and we've almost run out of time for dealing with it. What we do now—work together, share information, set other wants and priorities aside, let our business contacts and our government leaders know that this is an issue that must be on the top of their lists every day (not just for the duration of an occasional speech)—determines what kind of world we're living in after New Year's Day 2000.

Whether we can share honest information and work together on this problem seems to me to be the make-or-break question, when it comes to the year 2000. A Y2K expert said to me recently, "The old way, the I'm-going-to-sue-you way, won't work with this issue." I absolutely agree. If the Pentagon can share sensitive missile-launch information with the former Soviet Union to make sure we're safe from year 2000 malfunctions, it seems to me businesses should be able to let their defenses down long enough to share the information that can save their partners from serious setbacks—or worse.

Beyond that, the best we can do is stay flexible, stay informed, and work for the best but prepare for the worst as much as is reasonably possible. And hang on. Because it's going to be an interesting ride.

Notes

1. Michael Noer, "One Million Reasons," *Forbes* (March 12, 1998).
2. Peter de Jager, "Moving to Zero," www.year2000.com (September 1998).

A YEAR 2000 GLOSSARY

How to Talk Techie

You should not need this glossary to read *Surviving the Computer Time Bomb*. I've avoided technical terms wherever possible and explained them wherever necessary. Also, I am not including basic computer terms such as *hardware* or *interface* on the assumption that most readers are familiar with them.

Instead, this glossary defines some common terms that you may encounter if you read other works about the year 2000 problem, attend a Y2K conference, or try to discuss this matter with technical people.

aging

Moving software forward in time to see how it functions in the year 2000.

assembler

An older computer language.

bridge

Software that allows non-year 2000-compliant systems to communicate with compliant ones. Bridges must be "built" between these two types of systems and then "burned" when the noncompliant system is brought into compliance.

C, C++

Computer languages.

client/server

A modern computer "architecture," in which several desktop computers are linked together by a local area network (LAN), and software used by all resides on a central file server. This technology has been replacing mainframes and mid-size computers in many organizations. Though many people assume that client/server programs are too new to contain year 2000 glitches, most of them do.

COBOL

An out-of-date computer language. Despite its obsolescence, it was once very prevalent, and there is more COBOL in use among the world's business computers than any other language. For this reason, most year 2000 repair efforts are to some extent focusing their attention on COBOL.

code

The actual words and symbols that instruct computers in programs.

compiler

A program that translates human-readable programming instructions into a machine-executable program.

compliance

The ability of software and hardware to function properly when faced with dates in or after the year 2000. Though this is a very general definition, most corporate year 2000 projects could benefit from a more specific one. For instance, does the program need to work properly in every possible situation? How many years into the future does it need to work?

DASD

An acronym for "direct access storage device"; refers to any memory storage device, such as a disk.

data expansion

Another name for field expansion.

date coding

A rarely used formula for achieving year 2000 compliance without expanding two-digit year fields to four-digit year fields. It assigns a value to every day, starting with January 1, 1900, which is day one. By this measure, January 1, 1998, is day 35,796, and January 1, 2000, is 36,526. Notice that it is possible to accurately identify dates within the current six-digit limits. But the problems and confusion this creates rarely make it worth the effort.

date field

The place in a program where a date is inserted, whether by a user, the computer's own calendar, or some other outside source.

distributed systems

A system of individual personal computers linked together by a local area network (LAN), as opposed to a mainframe, which is not distributed.

enterprise

A term used by IT people typically to refer to an organization, or to the separate divisions or business units within that organization.

environment

The type of computer and operating system on which programs run, such as mainframe environment or client/server environment.

event horizon

The time that something begins happening. When referring to the year 2000 problem, it is the time when Y2K-related malfunctions begin to occur.

field expansion

Expanding programs so that two-digit date fields become four-digit date fields ("1999" instead of "99"). This is the most expensive way to solve a year 2000 problem, though it also offers the most permanent and unambiguous result.

FORTRAN

An old computer language widely used in scientific and technical settings.

Hollerith card

A feature of early computing. Programming instructions were hole punched on eighty-column cards that were then fed into the computer. Depending on how old you are, how long you've been using computers, and how good your memory is, you may remember encountering these. This is where the year 2000 problem arose: Using four-digit years with technology like this would have been prohibitively expensive and hugely inefficient.

interpretation
See *windowing.*

LAN
An acronym for local area network. LANs typically link several personal computers within an organization.

legacy
Older computer systems that we have inherited from the past.

logic
Logic means what you think it does, but because of how computer programs work (using logic to follow from one instruction to another and execute their given commands) this is sometimes used to refer to such things as IF . . . THEN instructions.

logic partition, or "L-Par"
Creation of an artificial partition in a mainframe computer, to set dates on part of the computer ahead to the year 2000 for software testing.

logic-based
See *windowing.*

masking
See *windowing.*

migration
Moving software or data from one computer system to another, often from an old, noncompliant system to a new, compliant one.

PASCAL
An older computer language.

pivot point
In windowing-type year 2000 solutions, the pivot point is the point at which the computer assumes a year is in the twentieth rather than the twenty-first century.

platform
Though sometimes used interchangeably with environment, platform refers to the type of hardware on which a program runs.

procedural

See *windowing.*

regression testing

Retesting a program after alteration (such as a year 2000 conversion) to make sure that the new adjustments have not affected its functioning.

repository

A core collection of software, usually stored in a database.

scope creep

Expanding the parameters of a project (such as adding on a systems upgrade to a year 2000 conversion) to better justify its cost. Scope creep is a big problem for most Y2K projects, which may already have trouble meeting their original goals in time to prevent malfunctions.

silver bullet

Yet-to-be-invented software that would provide a complete, foolproof, error-free solution to the entire year 2000 problem with little or no human effort. Like the yeti, the silver bullet is believed to be out there somewhere, even though there are no reliable eyewitness accounts of its existence.

source code

The instructions for a program, written by a programmer in COBOL or another computer language. Source code is then translated by a compiler into machine code that actually drives the computer when the program runs. Missing source code presents a huge problem for year 2000 conversion efforts, since it's impossible to rewrite a program from machine code alone. Some kind of (usually costly) reconversion is needed first.

spaghetti code

A thicket of IF . . . THEN and GOTO statements so tangled that it's impossible to tell where they begin and end.

test bed

A computer system that can be made to simulate an actual working environment. Programs that have been rewritten for year 2000 compliance should be checked on a test bed before they are put to actual use.

tool

A piece of software that helps programmers work on programs. There are many useful tools on the market that can help programmers make year 2000 adjustments more efficiently.

triage

The process of determining which of your systems have priority for year 2000 repairs, and which can be allowed to fail without threatening your organization's survival. This term was originally used on battlefields to determine which wounded soldiers should receive scarce medical care.

UNIX

A newer, language-based operating system in use on many computers. It is particularly suited to multiuser tasks.

windows, windowing

Also called procedural, interpretation, and logic-based, this is a way of making a program year 2000-compliant without the fuss of expanding its year field from two to four digits. Instead, the programmer estimates a "window" of time within which dates are deemed to be in the twenty-first, rather than the twentieth, century. In short, the last two digits of a year determine what the first two should be. For instance, two-digit years of 49 or less become 20xx, while all years with a value of 50 or more become 19xx. This is a much less expensive, though less permanent, solution than field expansion. The pivot point, where the century changes, can be fixed or sliding. For example, it can change according to the current date. Because windowing is quicker and less expensive than field expansion, it is gaining ascendance as the most common year 2000 solution. (The terms *window* and *windowing* bear no relation to the various Microsoft Windows products that run on personal computers.)

RECOMMENDED OTHER READING

Want to Know More?

Peter de Jager and Richard Bergeon, *Managing 00: Surviving the Year 2000 Computing Crisis* (John Wiley & Sons, 1997)

A fun, friendly book, it gives advice on addressing the year 2000 problem within your organization, as well as information on the various types of available software tools.

Capers Jones, *The Year 2000 Software Problem: Quantifying the Costs and Assessing the Consequences* (Addison Wesley, 1997)

Jones has done a great deal of research to put the year 2000 glitch into quantifiable terms; this book consists of both an overview of the problem and a series of tables showing Y2K's probable effect, by industry, by size of company, by country, and so on. Very useful for anyone trying to get a handle on the dimensions of the problem.

William M. Ulrich and Ian S. Hayes, *The Year 2000 Software Crisis: Challenge of the Century* (Prentice Hall, 1997)

Ulrich and Hayes, *The Year 2000 Software Crisis: The Continuing Challenge* (Prentice Hall, 1998)

These books offer comprehensive, detailed information on dealing with Y2K from both technical and management points of view.

Ed Yourdon and Jennifer Yourdon, *Time Bomb 2000: What the Year 2000 Computer Crisis Means to You!* (Prentice Hall, 1998)

This book looks at what some of the direst results of the year 2000 glitch could be. It's highly readable and written entirely for laypeople, and the Yourdons give useful advice on how to prepare for loss of essential services for varying lengths of time.

Year/2000 Journal, Marbo Enterprises, Inc., P.O. Box 550547, Dallas, TX 75355-0547; tel (214) 349-2147, fax (214) 341-7081; online at www.y2kjournal.com

This bimonthly journal is full of interesting articles and helpful information from numerous year 2000 professionals. Most (though not all) can be easily understood by nontechnical readers. Short sidebar comments from corporate executives at work on the year 2000 are particularly interesting.

Useful World Wide Web Pages

Year 2000 issues are constantly changing, and one of the best ways to keep track of them is by checking in with some of the Web pages devoted to this issue. Here are a few of the best.

www.itaa.com

The Information Technology Association of America's home page. Sign up here for ITAA's weekly Y2K e-mail newsletter, which tracks the latest year 2000 developments.

www.y2knews.com

Want to know the latest year 2000 headlines from around the world? This is the place to go; the page offers links to all the latest news stories.

www.yardeni.com

Ed Yardeni, economist at Deutsche Bank Securities, is (at this writing) the only economist attempting to project what the ultimate effects of Y2K might be. Fortunately, he's a lively writer who has put many of his conclusions into an online "Netbook." The book, along with his publication *Y2K Reporter,* can be accessed through his Website. The freely downloadable software Adobe Acrobat Reader is needed for *Y2K Reporter*.

www.year2000.com

This is Peter de Jager's Website, the Year 2000 Information Center. It contains links to many useful writings by de Jager and other Y2K experts, job listings, and a general forum on the subject. There are also masterfully compiled—and searchable!—archives of news reports and other information on every possible aspect of Y2K. In addition, the pages publish an e-mail newsletter that can help keep you informed.

Others:

www.wsrcg.com

This is consultant Warren S. Reid's Web site, which includes useful articles on Y2K.

Phillips, Charles E., and Farrell, William. *Y2K Watch: Digital Plague Oozes Across Planet.* Morgan Stanley, (March 26, 1997)

This 30-page article is well-written and fun. It contains some comments from programmers who helped create the year 2000 problem and gives a great overview of the issue. As well, it gives some predictions of which vendors are likely to be good investments.

INDEX

About the Author

Minda Zetlin is a freelance writer who specializes in business management and technology. She is the author of *The Computer Time Bomb: How to Keep the Century Date Change from Killing Your Organization* (American Management Association, 1997). She is a regular contributor to the AMA magazine *Management Review,* as well as *Nation's Business, Cosmopolitan, Games,* and many others. She also covers technology in emerging markets for the IBM Web magazine *Other Voices.*

Zetlin lives in Woodstock, New York, with her partner Bill Pfleging, a large number of computers, and four cats.

She can be contacted at MindaZ@aol.com or http://members.aol.com/MindaZ.